The Green Engineer

Engineering Careers to Save the Earth

BY CELESTE BAINE

Engineering Education
Service Center

Eugene, OR

The Green Engineer
Engineering Careers to Save the Earth

by Celeste Baine

Published by:
Engineering Education Service Center (imprint of Bonamy Publishing)
1004 5th Street
Springfield, OR 97477 U.S.A.
(541) 988-1005
www.engineeringedu.com

Printed in the United States of America.

Publishers Cataloging-in-Publication
Baine, Celeste
        The green engineer. Engineering careers to save the earth.
        p.   cm
Includes bibliographical references
        ISBN 978-0-9819300-8-4 (pbk.)
        1. engineering—vocational guidance. 2. career education—handbooks, manuals, etc. 3. engineering—study and teaching
        4. green engineering—vocational guidance. "HIGHER". I. Title.
        II. Baine, Celeste.

How to Order:
Single copies may be ordered from the Engineering Education Service Center, 1004 5th Street, Springfield, OR 97477; telephone (541) 988-1005. Web site: engineeringedu.com. Quantity discounts are also available.

The pages of this book are printed on 30% post consumer recycled paper using soy based inks.

This book is dedicated to Amy and her pursuit for a better world.

Acknowledgments

My peer reviewers were shining stars on a dark night. This book wouldn't be the same without their helpful sights, encouraging comments and depth of knowledge. Thank you Lisa Freed, Gay Taylor, and Amy Siddon.

I'd also like to thank the engineers that took the time to complete my surveys and patiently answered my questions. I'm deep in debt to your hospitality. In particular, I want to thank Gay Taylor, Philip Boutelle, Kellie Stokes, Abena Sackey Ojetayo and Conchita Jimenez-Gonzalez for their generosity and willingness to talk about their careers.

My thanks and gratitude also goes out to all the amazing people on the WEPAN listserve. Thank you for always connecting me to such amazing engineers!

Contents

About this book

Green engineering looks to the future and also corrects the past. As our technological abilities have advanced, many inventions have harmed our environment, ecological systems, and people. Burning fossil fuels contributes to global climate change, and creates toxins that have destroyed ecosystems. Damming rivers to harvest hydropower has endangered many types of fish. Creating a society used to disposable goods has created mountains of trash and an ocean full of plastics.

Green engineering is about designing a more thoughtful future—one that considers people and a healthy planet as much as the bottom line. Green engineers work hard to protect our scarce natural resources and care deeply about all of the creatures that inhabit our fragile world.

The information compiled in this guide will help you explore green engineering. The opportunities available for engineers in this industry are as varied as the engineers themselves. Engineers trained in civil, mechanical, electrical, chemical, manufacturing, marine, ocean, and software engineering (among others) make a difference everyday in their fields. But, one of the most rewarding aspects of being a green engineer is that you can make a difference right away—from the first day on the job through the rest of your career. Because sustainability is greatly needed, green engineering is a fast-growing field that offers a chance to protect the health and safety of people and our planet.

Green engineers are:
- Designing cleaner car engines for improved efficiency as well as electric, fuel cell, and hybrid vehicles.
- Working to improve the efficiency of wind, water, geothermal, biomass and solar power.
- Looking for ways to put solar cells into the paint of cars so that electric cars never need to be plugged in.
- Creating solar windows for houses and office buildings.

- Designing new electric car batteries that last longer on extended drives.
- Creating airplanes that can run on algae instead of fossil fuels.
- Developing manufacturing plants that run on biomass-generated power.
- Designing green buildings that have the capability to power themselves.
- Creating better packaging for consumer goods – reducing waste.
- Creating the infrastructure and means for impoverished countries to have access to clean water, electricity and internet services.
- And much more.

From renewable energy to preventing pollution. From assessing the environmental and social impact of products, services and goods, to recycling methods and from green transportation to green building design, these earth friendly professionals concern themselves with preventing and correcting problems caused by industrialization. They concentrate on delivering better environmental conditions for the public through knowledge, research, a caring attitude, and common sense.

You would enjoy a career in green engineering if you want to work with people, help make a more sustainable future, and are interested in saving the planet. Green engineering is a booming field, and more jobs will be created because our planet needs environmentally sustainable solutions to support population growth and preserve our limited natural resources. More energy from wind, solar, biofuel, and wave sources is needed, and there is increased demand for green buildings, food, improved technologies, and transportation systems.

Companies that employ green engineers are everywhere! Engineering firms, NASA, government agencies (such as the Department of Energy, the Department of Agriculture, and the

Environmental Protection Agency) all hire green engineers. Many large firms also employ green engineers to work to reduce their environmental footprint. Some build, design, or inspect green-energy systems, and others develop and administer the regulations that protect health, safety, and the environment.

One of the best things about being a green engineer is that you can study almost any type of engineering. The most common engineering majors are agricultural and biological, environmental, civil, mechanical, materials, electrical, and chemical engineering. A person trained as a mechanical engineer might help design wind turbines, and an electrical engineer may work for a company that designs solar panels.

Because engineering is a constantly changing process, it is more like a journey than a destination. Engineers constantly strive to make things better. They may develop technology that can be used to power our homes today but they don't stop there. The next week, they may be working on improving a design, or they may have a new idea about how to harvest energy more efficiently.

A career in engineering is never boring! For most engineers, the ideas don't stop once a product is designed. There are always improvements that can be made. Some improvements happen because there is new technology or systems available, and some improvements happen because the needs of society have changed.

Don't forget that many of the jobs you may see in the next 10 years haven't even been invented yet. Many up and coming engineers will not only create new products but new engineering sectors as well. Biomimicry alone offers numerous possibilities for building design, ventilation systems, electrical systems and many other things. Biomass opens up a whole host of possibilities for new fuels, paints, solvents, finishes, and other products to replace chemically produced products that are toxic. Sustainable solutions range from very simple things like using fast growth bamboo for hardwood in buildings rather than cutting down much slower growing trees that help clean the air, to recently announced buildings that "breathe" by circulating fresh air. Get your degree, get some experience, and be ready. Engineers are leading the way to making the world a better place. The possibilities are endless for a motivated student.

Green engineers are saving the world!

Chapter 1

Power and Energy Engineering

We use energy every day. Not only do we use energy to walk, talk, play sports, and function, but we also use energy to power our cars, toast our bread, watch TV, and charge our cell phones. Energy is everywhere and there are multiple forms of it. Energy can be electrical, chemical, thermal, geothermal, nuclear, light, kinetic, sound, potential, or hydro. In order to solve our energy crisis, we must learn how to convert these forms into electrical energy (electricity).

According to the Central Intelligence Agency, the United States consumed 18.7 million barrels of oil per day in 2009. Oil is a fossil fuel, along with coal and natural gas. At one time, fossil fuels were a great source of energy because they were cheap, plentiful, and easily transported. However when fossil fuels are burned (all fossil fuels must be burned to release the energy), they release carbon dioxide into the atmosphere. This pollution/ greenhouse gas is a major contributor to global climate change and the greenhouse effect.

We know that global climate change is occurring. According to NASA, the evidence that suggests it includes:

- The levels of atmospheric carbon dioxide are higher today than at any time in the past. Scientists reconstructed past climate conditions through evidence in tree rings, coral reefs, and ice cores. Ice cores from two miles deep in the Antarctic contain tiny atmospheric air bubbles that date back as far as 650,000 years. These samples have allowed

11

scientists to construct a historical record of greenhouse gas concentrations stretching back thousands of years.

- The global sea level rose about 17 centimeters (6.7 inches) in the 20th century. The rate of rise in the last decade, however, is nearly double that of the last century.
- All three major global surface temperature measurements have increased since 1880. Most of this warming has occurred since 1981 with the 10 warmest years occurring in the last 12 years.
- The oceans have absorbed most of this heat with significant portions of ocean showing a warming of 0.302 degrees Fahrenheit since 1969. With a rise in the overall temperature of the ocean, tropical storms and hurricanes could increase in force.

Developing sources of renewable energy is critical because one day, we will run out of oil. Renewable energy types include solar, wind, ocean, hydropower, hydrogen, biomass, and geothermal. When an energy source is renewable, it can be reused with little or no strain on our natural resource supplies. For example, energy from the sun can provide power when it hits a solar panel. The sun's energy is renewable because the energy from the sun is still available even after you use it. Power provided by natural gas is non-renewable because once you burn the gas, it is gone  forever. Renewable energy technologies are also clean sources of energy and better for the environment. Continuing to rely heavily on fossil fuels will limit our energy independence and our access to clean water and clean air.

Researching and harvesting renewable energy can:
- Protect our environment and public health by avoiding or reducing emissions that contribute to smog, acid rain, and global climate change.

- Increase economic development and create new green-collar jobs.
- Create more competition to help restrain fossil fuel price increases.
- Diversify our fuel sources and enhance the reliability of fuel supplies.
- Insulate our economy from fossil fuel price spikes and supply shortages or disruptions.
- Reduce a growing reliance on imported fuel and electricity.
- Reduce the cost of complying with present and future environmental regulations.
- And conserve our natural resources for future generations.

It's impossible to separate the future of careers in green engineering from the future of the planet. Every career depends on what the future may hold, but green careers are more sensitive to changes in the world. Fortunately, because the world is moving toward increased sustainability and rebuilding and conserving our natural resources, the future looks very bright for green engineers. The opportunities offer a challenging and satisfying chance to protect the health and safety of people and the planet.

Solar Energy Engineering

Solar energy comes from the sun. Imagine that you are sitting inside a car or lying on the grass and the sun is shining. The sun is providing light and heat energy, too. Over the years, engineers have found many ways to capture the sun's heat and light to benefit people. Solar technology can be simple or complicated, and small-scale for home use or large-scale for industry. However, the one thing that all the systems have in common is that they provide a reliable alternative source of electricity, improve efficiency, and also save money.

In 2010, the majority of the electricity used around the world came from fossil fuels, which are not renewable and in limited supply. This limited supply drives up the cost, makes us dependent on the countries that have significant supplies and can lead to war. It's very important for engineers to develop solar technologies because unlike the burning of fossil fuels, after development, solar energy has no emissions. Using solar energy can improve our air quality and reduce the possibility of global climate change caused by greenhouse gas emissions. Fortunately, engineers have been hard at work creating many different systems to collect the sun's energy.

Some of the solar-energy technologies that have been developed include:

- Solar cells and panels—Solar panels convert sunlight into electricity.
- Concentrating solar power systems—Concentrating solar power (CSP) technologies use mirrors to reflect and concentrate sunlight onto receivers that collect solar energy and convert it to heat. This thermal (heat) energy can then be used to produce electricity with a steam turbine or heat engine that drives a generator. In other words, CSP systems convert solar energy into heat to create electricity. These systems allow power plants to produce electricity on a large scale so that consumers can purchase solar electricity without having a personal system in their home.
- Passive solar heating—Passive solar heating uses solar energy to heat and light buildings. This can help homes and buildings become more efficient and comfortable.
- Solar hot water systems—Solar hot water systems heat water through a series of tubes on the roof with solar energy.
- Solar collecting paints—Solar collecting paints convert sunlight into electricity.

According to the US Department of Energy, adding solar energy to our nation's energy mix:

- provides America with clean and diversified sources of energy supply,
- increases energy security by moving away from large centralized power plants,
- reduces the need for new conventional power plants,
- improves our environment by avoiding greenhouse gas emissions,
- improves the quality of air we breathe,
- stimulates our economy and creates jobs by promoting a U.S.-based solar industry, and
- creates an easy-to-deploy, mobile energy supply for emergencies, disasters, and national defense purposes.

Adding solar technologies to homes and property:

- improves property values,
- saves money on electricity bills,
- provides a hedge against future energy price increases,
- provides security by using an energy source that is unlimited,
- creates a sustainable energy future, and
- provides an uninterrupted energy supply during blackouts with the use of batteries for power backup and energy storage, and
- eases the pressure on an aging electrical grid.

Adding solar technologies to businesses:

- provides positive financial returns (solar energy projects can generate positive cash flow immediately based on green financing options),
- creates no emissions or noise,
- provides a hedge against future energy price increases,
- provides energy supply to remote installations or buildings,

- creates a mobile energy supply for use in emergencies and disasters, and
- provides an uninterrupted energy supply during blackouts with the use of batteries for power backup and energy storage.

Utility companies benefit because solar energy:
- reduces or avoids the need to build new transmission/ distribution lines or upgrade existing ones,
- helps meet peak power needs,
- diversifies the range of energy sources in use and increase the reliability of the grid network,
- can be installed in small increments to match the requirements of the customer,
- provides a potential revenue source in a diverse energy portfolio,
- helps meet renewable sources goals, and
- helps off-set or avoid carbon emissions.

Another advantage of solar energy is that when a homeowner installs solar panels and the panels produce more electricity than the homeowner needs, the extra can be sold to the utility company (as of this writing, most but not all utility companies will purchase electricity from their customers).

The challenge for solar energy engineers is to make solar energy more efficient and affordable. The efficiency of a solar panel is how well it converts sunshine into usable electricity. Because of Newton's 2nd law, we know that energy cannot be created or destroyed, only changed into another form. Back in the 1950's, when solar panels were first produced, they were only 4 percent efficient. In other words, they could only convert 4 percent of the sunshine that was hitting them into electricity. Ninety-six percent of the sun's energy was either reflected back into the atmosphere or absorbed by the materials that made up the solar cells. In 2006, after tremendous research by many scientists and engineers, panels increased to 15 percent efficiency. At the time of this writing, the most efficient solar panel is made by Alta Devices and is 23.5 percent efficient. However, research is being conducted that may lead to panels of 50 percent or greater efficiency. Although that sounds amazing, engineers must always balance the cost with the environmental impact of using new materials or technologies.

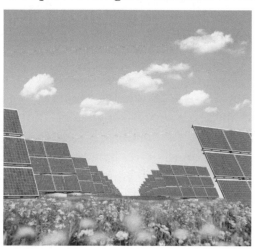

SOLAR CELLS AND PANELS

Solar cells, also called photovoltaics, are made of semiconducting materials similar to those used in computer chips. When sunlight is absorbed by these materials, the solar energy knocks electrons loose from their atoms, allowing the electrons to flow through the material to produce electricity. This process of converting light (photons) to electricity is called the photovoltaic (PV) effect.

About 40 solar cells are placed together to form a module. About 10 modules form an array. An array is what we call a solar panel. Panels are usually installed facing South at a fixed angel, or on a sun-tracking device that follows the path of the sun. Panels will convert the most sunshine to electricity when they are perpendicular to the sun. Because the angle of the sun changes with the time of day, panels should be adjusted accordingly. Large panels made up of 10 to 20 PV arrays can provide enough power for one household.

In addition to regular solar cells, engineers and scientists have also developed thin film solar cells. Just like the name implies, the layers of semiconductor materials are only a few micrometers thick. Having such thin material allows the solar cells to double as rooftop shingles, roof tiles, building facades, or glazing for skylights.

Solar cells or photovoltaic systems are designed, manufactured, and installed by electrical, mechanical, manufacturing, materials and civil engineers. The type of engineer determines the role they play in the process. Most often, electrical engineers will work on the circuitry, materials engineers will develop the materials, civil engineers will find a site and make sure the panels are mounted securely, and manufacturing engineers will work on the production of the panels. Every engineer works to make the systems more efficient and affordable. And, it takes a team of engineers to make a project successful.

Concentrating Solar Power

Concentrating solar power (CSP) technologies use mirrors to reflect and concentrate sunlight onto receivers that collect solar energy and convert it to heat. This thermal energy can then be used to produce electricity with a steam turbine or heat engine that drives a generator. In other words, CSP systems convert solar energy into heat to create electricity. These systems allow power plants to produce electricity on a large scale so that consumers can purchase solar electricity without having a personal system in their home.

There are three main types of CSP systems:

1. Parabolic-trough—Parabolic-trough systems have long rectangular, curved (U-shaped) mirrors. The mirrors are tilted toward the sun, focusing sunlight on a pipe that runs down the center of the trough. This can heat anything that is in the pipe. To produce electricity, oil flows through the pipe that, when heated, is then used to boil water in a conventional steam generator.

2. Dish/Engine—A dish/engine system looks like the large satellite dishes used for televisions except that it uses a mirrored dish-shaped surface to collect and concentrate the sun's heat onto a receiver. The receiver absorbs the heat and heats a fluid within the engine. When the fluid heats up, it expands and turns a turbine. (Remember Newton's law. In this case, the heat is being converted to mechanical energy). The turning turbine is connected to a generator or alternator that produces electricity.

3. Power Tower—If you have ever driven by a large field of mirrors, you have passed a power tower. A power tower system uses a large field of mirrors that concentrate all of the sun's energy to a receiver, which usually sits on top of a tower. Molten salt (a salt that retains heat very well) flows through the receiver and the salt's heat generates electricity through a conventional steam generator. Because of this special salt, heat can be stored for days in the receiver before being converted into electricity. This enables electricity to be produced on cloudy days or even after sunset.

PASSIVE SOLAR HEATING

A well designed passive solar house will stay warm in the winter and cool in the summer. Houses that are designed to take advantage of passive solar heating and daylighting usually have large, South-facing windows. These structures use materials for the floors and walls that absorb and store the solar energy. The floors and walls heat up during the day, and slowly release the heat at night when temperatures drop.

Solar energy can be active or passive:

* Active solar heating is when you use electrical or mechanical means to warm air or water.
* Passive solar heating uses the floors, walls, and windows to collect, store, and use the heat from the sun to warm air or water. The system warms the house in the winter and cools the house in the summer. In addition to solar heating, a passive solar house can also provide natural lighting.

According to *The Passive Solar House* by James Kachadorian, there are 10 principles to passive solar design:
1. Orient the house properly with respect to the sun's relationship to the site.
2. Design on a 12-month basis.
3. Provide effective thermal mass to store free solar heat in the daytime for nighttime use.
4. Insulate thoroughly and use well-sealed vapor barriers.
5. Utilize windows as solar collectors and cooling devices.
6. Prevent overglazing.
7. Avoid oversizing the backup heating system or air-conditioning.
8. Provide fresh air to the home without compromising thermal integrity.
9. Use the same material you would use for a conventional home, but in ways that maximize energy efficiency and solar gain.
10. Remember that the principles of solar design are compatible with diverse styles of architecture and building techniques.

Based on the list above, it should be clear that a large part of civil and architectural engineering is about understanding the properties of materials. A passive solar house requires materials that are good for thermal mass and insulation. Thermal mass acts as a heat storage device and provides a way to store solar heat for use later when the sun has gone down. Insulation is required to hold the heat (thermal energy) in winter and release the heat in summer.

SOLAR HOT WATER SYSTEMS

Solar hot water systems usually sit on a rooftop and face South. Most systems consist of a solar collector, a series of tubes that carry the water or fluid to be heated, and a storage tank that stores the hot water. When the sun warms a lake, the surface and shallow parts of the lake heat up first. The same is true for a solar hot water heater. Small quantities of water make its way through the series of tubes and pass an "absorber plate" that is positioned to absorb heat from the sun. The absorber plate is black in color to promote optimal heat absorption. As heat builds up on the absorber plate, the fluid that is passing through the tubes is significantly warmed.

There are two kinds of solar hot water systems:
1. Active—Active systems rely on pumps to move the liquid in the tubes from the solar collector to the storage tank and back again.
2. Passive—Passive systems use gravity and convection to circulate the water.

A homeowner may also tie the solar water heater to an electricity or gas-powered system for additional heat in the winter. However, by reducing the amount of heat required from a regular water heating system, homeowners can reduce their electricity or fossil fuel usage by as much as 80 percent.

To help with research, the US Department of Energy began a program called the Solar Energy Technologies Program. This program focuses on developing cost-effective solar energy technologies that have the greatest potential to benefit our nation and the world. Their tagline really says it all, "Bringing you a prosperous future where energy is clean, abundant, reliable and affordable." Our nation's success in the solar industry means that everyone will live more comfortably.

SOLAR COLLECTING PAINTS

Solar collecting paints are currently being developed that can conduct electricity when the thermal energy from the sun comes in contact with the paint. This special paint can be brushed on a house or car to easily allow that house or car to generate electricity. In a research project called, "Sun-Believable", researchers at Notre Dame University said that although the paint is not available yet, it may one day be able to be turn your house into a massive solar-powered generator.

The paint is made from tiny particles of titanium dioxide coated with one or two cadmium-based substances, mixed with a water-alcohol mixture to create a paste. The drawback is that the best light-to-energy conversion efficiency reached so far is 1 percent, which is well behind the usual 10 to 15 percent efficiency of commercial silicon solar cells. However, if the efficiency can be improved, it may be able to make a real difference in meeting our energy needs in the future because the paint can be made inexpensively and in large quantities.

AN INTERVIEW WITH PHILIP BOUTELLE, MECHANICAL ENGINEER FOR AN ENERGY NON-PROFIT

1. How did you first learn about your field? Was it your intention to have a "green" career?

    It was my intention to get a green career. When I first decided to go back to college (at age 26), I knew that I wanted to work in something environmental. I thought about various career paths I could follow and the degrees that would best support my personal strengths and interests, and decided that engineering would be the best fit. I liked that it was challenging, involved math and problem-solving, and allowed for a huge range of job types once I was done with school. During my second year of community college, I got a part time job at a solar installation company doing design work, and that helped solidify my sights on a job in solar. I worked in solar for about 5.5 years, then got into my current job at the non-profit. Now, my company contracts with utilities to help commercial customers reduce energy consumption on their buildings.

2. Where did you go to school? What kind of degree do you have?

    I first attended Cabrillo College in Aptos, CA, and earned my Associates of Science degree in Engineering. I then transferred to San Jose State University, and earned a Bachelor's of Science in Mechanical Engineering, Summa Cum Laude, with a focus on thermal fluid sciences.

3. What do you do now? What is your day like?

    I spend some time in the field doing energy audits and engineering support for sales, and the rest of the time in the office working out the calculations to back up our claims, and putting the results of our calculations into presentable documents/reports. However, we're a relatively small company, so I wear a lot of hats. I spend some of my time on internal process improvements, with a goal of making our processes easier to scale. I provide support to our divisions that don't require as much hands-on engineering but still need occasional technical input, and I get involved in development work as well. My job is perfect because it is challenging, different every day, and my company has the same environmental goals that I have. I work with a senior engineer who has been working in energy efficiency for a long time, so I learn a lot every day and I'm constantly improving as an engineer. One interesting thing about the change in jobs: at first, it was hard to really be proud of my current job; I came from solar, which was so marketable, and in many senses the most 'sexy' green job out there. But once I saw the environmental statistics about reducing energy (versus generating energy), I was completely on board. I'm a little over a year into my 'new' job, and I can't imagine doing anything else.

4. What advice do you have for students that are interested in becoming a green engineer? Do you recommend it? What skills are most important to be good at your job?

    A lot of students think that when you want to be a green engineer, you need to study solar or wind or something specific, but that view is a little misguided. Any engineer can be a green engineer. It matters less what specific engineering discipline someone studies but more about their individual principles. Green engineering is everywhere and applicable to every environmental discipline, either in specific applications or in broad environmental terms. For example, an electrical engineer could work on a specific technology (that is, solar cells or a better light bulb), or they could work on improving the overall efficiency of circuits or larger scale power transmission. A civil engineer could work on improving building techniques to minimize material usage, or design a better dam that doesn't inhibit fish from reproducing. Even a nuclear engineer could be designing safer and cleaner ways to decommission nuclear plants and weapons to minimize environmental damage. I could go on and on about the endless possibilities for 'green' engineering, and I recommend it 100%. The world would benefit from engineers being more deliberate with their choice of jobs and really tailoring their work towards what they believe in.

The skills required for success are the same in most engineering jobs: ability to learn from mistakes, excellent communication skills (written, verbal, and listening), organization, and a backbone of core engineering skills that any undergrad should be confident applying.

5. What's your favorite part of the job?

    As an environmentalist, I love that the work I do directly reduces energy consumption of our customers. Plus, it's close enough that I can ride my bike to work every day!

6. What is the worst part?

    Sometimes it's tough to wade through utility and regulator bureaucratic processes.

7. If you could do it all over again, what, if anything, would you change and why?

    I would have taken an internship at a different company every summer so I could try out more jobs and see what I liked and didn't like. It can be hard to discover your passion just by taking classes, and internships are easy ways to get a taste of a job or an industry. I would have also started working with a Registered Professional Engineer (P.E.) sooner (immediately upon graduation), so I could have been ready to take my own P.E. exam sooner as well.

THE ENGINEERS WHO HELP HARVEST SOLAR ENERGY

Besides the work described below, all engineers in the solar energy industry may work as consultants, advising home owners and businesses on the best type and size solar system. In addition, many engineers may find they enjoy sales, marketing, customer service or field installations. These descriptions are not rigid. Anyone of these engineers can do some or all of the things described in the other engineering disciplines.

- Civil and Structural Engineers may design buildings to most efficiently use the sun's energy. They may also be involved in site selection and the construction of solar plants.
- Computer Engineers may design smart grids and control systems to deliver energy more efficiently.
- Electrical Engineers and Electronic Engineers may develop the technology to generate, store, or distribute the renewable solar energy harvested. They may be responsible for grid connections, designing the transmission lines, and the logistics of transporting energy across land. They may design electrical, computer, and automation systems, alarms, and communication systems.
- Environmental Engineers may participate in the design, manufacturing, or installation of solar technology to protect people and the environment by evaluating and limiting toxic materials. They assess the processes used

during construction, and study the potential impact on ecosystems at the installation site, as well as water and air pollution from manufacturing or installation.

- Manufacturing and Industrial Engineers evaluate, troubleshoot, validate, and improve the manufacturing processes of solar cells and panels. They also work on new technologies and equipment to make the cells, panels, and any other systems to harvest the energy. They are responsible for all aspects of purchasing electronic and mechanical components and products.

- Materials and Chemical Engineers may research advanced materials that may improve the solar energy efficiency while also lowering cost and improving the stability of the integrated systems. They may also research new applications for solar cells, such as integrating them into windows or paint. They may also develop new solar collecting technology from new materials and processes.

- Mechanical Engineers may design energy and control systems, or they may build and test prototypes, make CAD models, or write and apply for patents. They may also provide installations, troubleshooting, or repair.

- Technicians may work in factory-authorized service centers. They are experienced in electronic repair, DC to AC conversion technology, and alternative energy systems. Technicians may also perform the set-up, calibration, testing, and troubleshooting of power inverters, instruments and electromechanical assemblies.

Wind Energy Engineering

Imagine for a moment that you are looking across a grassy field. One day, the field will be full of turbines, but you are in charge of installing the first one. How are you going to do it? A few of the things you would need to know are:

- The speed of the wind in different seasons so that you can determine how much structural load will be on the turbine (which will also help you determine the amount of energy the turbine should be producing).
- The direction of the wind for optimum placement.
- The optimal height of the wind to determine the height of the turbine.
- How much the turbine weighs.
- How far to drive the turbine base into the ground so it doesn't fall over in a big windstorm.
- How much concrete to pour into the ground to promote stability.
- The weather on the day of installation.
- How many parts need assembly and how they fit together (which will help you communicate with the crane operator).

Of course, these are a simplistic list of some of the coordination that engineers must do.

In 2009, the National Renewable Energy Laboratory (NREL) installed a 1.5 Megawatt (MW) wind turbine on its property. The turbine was 388.8 feet tall from the ground to the tip, 126.3 feet around, and weighed 300 tons. Engineers determined that it required 80 trucks of concrete to hold it up in all weather conditions.

In 2007, the average electricity used in a US home was 936 kilowatt-hours (kWh). The estimated production from this one wind turbine is 1,600,000 kWh/year, or enough to power 142 homes for a year. Because the NREL is a testing laboratory, these figures are considered low compared to a commercial wind farm.

The turbine installed was a horizontal axis turbine, and it is the most common type used today. It has a tower usually made up of three pieces that are stacked on top of each other. On top of the tower is a generator that turns when the blades rotate in the wind. There can be two or three blades, and they can face the wind or be turned away from it.

According to the Department of Energy, "Horizontal axis turbines sit high atop towers to take advantage of the stronger and less turbulent wind at 100 feet (30 meters) or more above ground. Each blade acts like an airplane wing, so when the wind blows, a pocket of low-pressure air forms on the downwind side of the blade. The low-pressure air pocket then pulls the blade toward it, which causes the rotor to turn. This is called lift. The force of the lift is actually much stronger than the wind's force against the front side of the blade, which is called drag. The combination of lift and drag causes the rotor to spin like a propeller, and the turning shaft spins a generator to make electricity."

Wind turbines are different from windmills. Although both use the wind to perform their tasks, windmills are used to pump water from an underground well or to grind grain, whereas wind turbines are used to produce electricity. Wind is a renewable resource and engineers design wind turbines to change the kinetic energy of the wind into mechanical and electrical energy.

Wind farms are usually found in regions that have strong and steady winds (most often in open fields, on top of mountains, or in the ocean). For most wind turbines to turn fast enough to generate  electricity, the wind must blow at a minimum of 12–14 miles per hour. To avoid damage to the blades, most turbines include a brake just in case the wind gets too strong.

Turbines rely on mechanical advantage and high gear ratios. When you look out into a wind farm, it always appears that the blades are turning slowly. Some wind turbine gear boxes have gear ratios of 100:1. That means that every time the blades make one revolution or turns in a complete circle (360 degrees), the gear turning the generator makes 100 revolutions! If a turbine runs at 12 RPM (turns 12 times in one minute), the inside gear is traveling at 1200 rotations per minute. As you can imagine, these speeds can produce friction and heat which cause the gears to require constant maintenance. Although that is good for keeping engineers and technicians employed, it can also get expensive. It would be more efficient to design a wind turbine that does not use gears at all, which is exactly what some engineers in the wind industry are trying to develop.

If installing a turbine doesn't sound exciting, there are other opportunities that engineers can access in the wind-energy industry. Engineers are also needed in:

- blade research, design, and manufacturing,
- turbine research, design, and manufacturing,
- energy storage so that you can use it later (like a battery),
- environmental assessment and site selection, and
- utility company grid integration.

Sometimes, assessing the environmental impact of wind turbines, a critical component for success, can unveil solutions to problems that weren't readily apparent. For example, a wind farm was constructed 25 years ago in California at the Altamont Pass (about 40 miles inland from San Francisco.) An impact study was conducted that reported that the turbines killed between 1766 and 4271 birds a year, including the federally protected golden eagle. Because newer turbines kill fewer birds (thanks to engineers that redesigned the blades) the turbine company NextEra, that built the older turbines, was forced to pay $2.5 million in mitigation fees and replace 2400 of the turbines in the pass.

Another study has revealed that a wind turbine's color affects how many insects it attracts. Researchers found that the turbines that were painted yellow, white or gray attracted insects and the least attractive color to the insects was purple. Because birds and bats feast on insects, this discovery of painting the turbines purple could provide a very cost-effective solution to saving thousands of birds and bats. However, other factors such as the heat generated by the turbine and the height of the blades could also play a determining factor.

In February of 2011, the US Department of the Interior and the US Fish and Wildlife Service issued voluntary guidelines for onshore wind energy developers to avoid harm to birds and other wildlife. As a result of these guidelines, bird migratory patterns are tracked as well as the impact to wildlife from and during wind farm site selection, construction, operation and maintenance.

Most jobs in the field of wind energy research require an electrical, computer, or mechanical engineering background. However, many other types of engineers, such as civil, manufacturing, environmental, aerospace and materials engineers are also involved. The challenges for engineers in this industry are how to make wind turbines more efficient and finding better ways to store or transport the electricity that is generated.

According to "Careers in Wind Energy" by Robin Arnette, the five major areas of wind energy research are:

- Turbine research—Involves research to improve turbine design (aerodynamics), understanding the nature of wind (inflow and turbulence), and using computer models to design efficient and low-cost turbines (modeling structures and dynamics).
- Wind resource assessment—Provides maps of a country or state/province that includes specific wind data such as average wind speed and its variability.
- Forecasting—Uses weather models (such as Doppler radar) to predict wind speeds and patterns at various altitudes. It also uses old data to predict how the wind will behave at a certain time.
- Utility grid integration—Integrates the energy produced by wind into a utility grid. New techniques and models will

ensure that grid operators can manage variable-output technologies like wind and solar with maximum efficiency.

- Energy storage—Uses technology to store wind energy as electricity. Some methods include converting it to chemical energy (like hydrogen), and flywheels.

Although the wind power industry is growing faster than any other renewable energy sector, it is also very competitive. So many people see it as a way to make a difference in the world and get in on the ground floor of a technology that will help shape the planet. According to Walter Sass, president and co-founder of SecondWind, a wind-energy monitoring company in Somerville, Massachusetts, wind energy is much more efficient than solar energy. "For the size of equipment, a modern wind turbine— typically 250 feet across, blade tip to blade tip—can generate a megawatt and a half to 2 megawatts at peak output," he says. "A similar sized solar panel array, which would be huge, would probably be five times as expensive in terms of how much area it's covering and produce a fraction of the power output."

According to Windforce 12, a study by the European Wind Energy Association (EWEA) and Greenpeace, employment in the wind sector could grow from approximately 114,000 jobs in 2001 to 1.47 million jobs in 2020 if wind energy meets 12% of the world's electricity needs. However, finding people with the right skills and expertise could prove a major constraint to the continued expansion of the industry and jeopardize the ability of many countries to meet their targets.

Vertical axis wind turbines are also progressing rapidly. These turbines are much smaller with a blade design that can take wind from any direction and convert it into energy. Some can use wind speeds as low as 5 mph and require less space than the big horizontal axis turbines. They can be mounted on rooftops in urban areas or the backyard of a residence. They can also be used in combination with solar panels for more opportunity for power generation.

According to Dayton Griffin, the Director of Engineering Research, Design, and Development at Global Energy Concepts in Seattle, Washington, "There are opportunities in blade production, tower production, or gearbox production and the electrical control systems would be electrical engineering." To set yourself apart from other candidates in this industry, there are several things that you can do to get the job first including:

1. Earn a degree from a college or university specializing in wind energy training.
2. Get a co-op or internship with a wind related company while in college.
3. Attend conferences and workshops in wind energy such as the Wind Energy Association. www.awea.org
4. Join a university lab whose focus is on wind research.
5. Get experience with the most commonly used wind analysis software such as WAsP, WindFarmer, WindFarm & WindPro.

It takes many people and companies to design, build, install, harvest from, and maintain wind turbines. Because wind energy engineers work closely with so many different people, it is very important to develop excellent communication skills such as public speaking and writing. You can choose to work in a small company on a niche product or you can work for a large utility company. The choices available are growing each day as more and more of the world begins to rely on green energy to meet its energy demands.

THE ENGINEERS WHO HELP HARVEST WIND ENERGY

- Aerospace Engineers may research ways to improve turbine aerodynamics while lowering the cost. They also study the nature of wind (inflow and turbulence), build and test prototypes, make CAD models, or write and apply for patents. However, all engineers could apply for patents.

- Electrical Engineers and Electronic Engineers may design electrical, computer and automation systems, alarms, and communication systems. They may also develop the technology to generate, store, or distribute the renewable energy harvested. They may be responsible for grid connections and designing the transmission lines.

- Civil and Structural Engineers may search for viable wind farm sites. They must understand land ownership issues, elicit community support, understand meteorological modeling and local grid infrastructure, as well as investigate if there can be accessible roads to the site and any possible transportation problems.

- Environmental Engineers participate in the design to protect people and the environment by limiting toxic materials. They also assess the processes used during construction and assess the site that will house the turbine to determine whether drinking water, sealife, plants, or animals will be affected by a new wind-power facility.

- Materials Engineers research advanced materials that may be able to withstand corrosion and storms while also lowering cost and improving the stability of the integrated systems.

- Mechanical Engineers may design specific items of machinery like cranes, hoists, elevators, and equipment for installing, anchoring, or moving the turbine structures and supplies. They may also manage the manufacturing processes for the turbines, gearboxes, towers, and blades and other technology. They may also research ways to improve turbine aerodynamics while lowering the cost.

Ocean Energy Engineering

As you read this, engineers are hard at work developing technologies that use the ocean and its resources to generate electricity. Energy from the ocean is most often renewable, and can help reduce our dependence on foreign oil. Even though ocean energy may provide enough energy to light the world in the future, it's important to minimize the disturbance that these technologies cause to the ocean floor and marine animals.

There are many ways to harvest energy from the ocean. The five you will read about below—wave energy converters, tidal energy devices, OTEC, ocean current converters, and offshore wind energy—are general methods of energy extraction. This list is not comprehensive and new methods and processes are being researched and developed continuously. There are many forms of energy extraction and several methods can also be used in rivers and lakes.

WAVE ENERGY CONVERTERS

Just like the name implies, this technology converts wave energy into electricity. Wave power can be harvested from oceans, gulfs, and lakes large enough to have waves that can be converted into electricity. Although it is a relatively new technology, it may hold the most promise because wave energy can be harnessed anywhere that holds this capability.

The technology can consist of:
- A buoy either on the water's surface or just below it that can capture the wave energy. The buoy system has a column that is filled with air. When a wave enters the buoy, the air in the column is forced upwards and the air turns a turbine. When the water recedes, the space left by the water creates a vacuum that also turns the turbine. In other words, the air

movement caused by the water moving up and down in the column turns the turbine which turns a motor to produce electricity. However, due to the relentless pounding of the waves and the corrosive nature of the ocean, these buoys often break or become nonfunctional, as seen off the Oregon coast where only 50% of all the buoys are in working order.

- Another technology is sea snake-looking device that is semi-submerged in the ocean. The "snake" generates power in the hinged joints that connect its sections. When a wave rolls by, the forward and back and side-to-side

Pelamis Wave Energy Converter.
Photo courtesy: Pelamis Wave Power Ltd.

swells activate hydraulic rams located in the hinges that pump high-pressure oil into hydraulic motors that drive electrical generators and produce electricity. The electricity is transported back to the shore in an underwater cable. Currently, this technology has been installed successfully as a 2.5 Megawatt wave farm off the coast of Portugal. A wave farm that takes up less space than a half square mile of ocean can generate 30 Megawatts of power, which is enough to power 20,000 homes.

TIDAL ENERGY DEVICES

A tidal energy device is just like a wind turbine except that it is underwater, and instead of wind, the current makes it turn. Just like the name implies, this type of system captures the energy of the tides or currents that run below the waves, and turns them into electricity. This is most often done by installing a turbine underwater that rotates in the current. The turbine may be bidirectional or may only be able to turn in one direction. In other words, some of these underwater turbines generate electricity only when the tide is going out, and some generate electricity when the tide is going out or coming into the shore.

These devices may be close to the shore or far out in the ocean. The ones submerged deep in the ocean are often strategically placed where the cold fresh waters from the poles meet the warmer, tropical waters that have absorbed more solar radiation. These areas create intense water circulation that has the potential to generate large amounts of electricity.

With these turbines, the amount of energy generated is directly proportional to the density of the fluid passing through them. Because water is much denser than air, a water turbine has several hundred times the power of an air turbine. On the flip side, the marine environment is so corrosive that repairs costs for underwater turbines can be substantial.

Ocean Thermal Energy Conversion (OTEC)

Ocean Thermal Energy Conversion, or OTEC, is like a big, slow heat pump. It only works if there is a 40 degree difference in the temperature of the surface water and the temperature of the water deep in the ocean. OTEC generates electricity by pumping the colder water from deep in the ocean into a heat exchanger. As you might have guessed, this technology is usually installed in island nations such as Hawaii and Puerto Rico. Forty floating OTEC power stations can generate enough electricity to power all of Puerto Rico forever.

To harvest the solar energy stored in the oceans, engineers have built an all-weather, hurricane-proof floating power station that uses the temperature difference to turn a turbine that generates electricity. The hot tropical water is used to boil a liquid such as propane that has a very low boiling temperature. The propane is turned into a gas that turns the turbine, which generates the electricity that is carried to land in an underwater cable. The cold

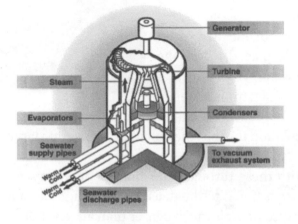

water of the deep ocean is then pumped into the heat exchanger where it cools and condenses the propane so that it can be turned back into a liquid and used again.

Think of it like this, 70 percent of the earth's surface is covered by water and 97 percent of that water is ocean water. In the tropical waters near the equator, the oceans can store 1000 times more heat than the atmosphere. That means that all of the heat (stored solar power) that is in the upper layers of the tropical oceans has the potential to supply more than 300 times the electrical needs of people on earth.

The additional benefit of this kind of energy generation is that it produces the useful by-product of fresh drinking water, and a supply of cool, nutrient-rich seawater that can be used to enhance such activities as mariculture (growing food in the ocean).

Ocean Current Energy

Ocean currents created by tides are generated from the gravitational attraction between the Earth and the Moon. High tide and low tide both occur twice a day and at regular intervals, so the direction of the current changes four times a day. Because of the regularity of the tides, the amount of energy that the current can generate can be estimated with accuracy. For example, current can travel at speeds of 10 knots or 11.5 miles per hour. Water traveling at 10 knots over an area of one square meter can generate up to 6 Kilowatts of power, or a little more than what is needed to power two houses.

There are also non-tidal ocean currents such as the Gulf Stream that are created by the solar heating of the tropical waters near the equator. Because hot water always cools down (Newton's law of thermodynamics), the hot tropical water makes its way North to the cold fresh waters of the Arctic. The rotation of the Earth, the salinity of the water, and the temperature differences that make the currents race are known as the "Coriolis Force."

Offshore Wind Energy

Offshore wind energy uses the same wind turbines as wind farms on land only they are in the ocean. Many other wind farms are in place all over the world, they are just not visible from the coastline.

In 2008, the Queen of England purchased the world's largest wind turbine for installation off Britain's shore. By 2012, the Queen's wind turbine will light up thousands of British homes. This turbine is so large it will tower over Big Ben, have a wingspan equivalent to two soccer fields, and will be able to produce 10 Megawatts of electricity, which is enough to power about 3,700 homes (a typical large turbine can only generate one fifth of that energy). This amount of clean energy will rid England of the need for two million barrels of oil, and 724,000 tons of carbon dioxide in the years it operates.

As you can imagine, engineers in this field have their hands full. Once all the parts of a turbine are manufactured, engineers have to figure out how to store, or distribute the renewable energy that is harvested. This can mean figuring out how to connect the turbines to the electrical grid, or designing transmission lines to transport the energy underwater and back to land. They design energy and control systems that can withstand corrosion, wave impacts, storms, and the constant motion of the ocean. And they also design the offshore wind turbine structures that are embedded in the ocean floor so that they can withstand hurricane winds, the weight of ice, and the impact of waves. They are also be responsible for mooring systems and running electrical cable underwater.

And don't forget all the technicians that do the actual installation and operation of specific items of machinery like cranes, hoists, elevators, and equipment for installing, anchoring, or moving structures and supplies—all this without getting seasick!

Ocean resources can meet a considerable proportion of our energy needs, and they can help alleviate many problems while providing other important benefits.

THE ENGINEERS WHO HELP HARVEST OCEAN ENERGY

- Aerospace Engineers may research ways to improve turbine aerodynamics while lowering the cost, study the nature of wind (inflow and turbulence), build and test prototypes, make CAD models, or write and apply for patents.
- Civil and Structural Engineers may specify the actual structure and mooring of the ocean energy technologies including framing, shell, foundations and anchoring. They ensure that the structures can withstand the weight of ice and the impact of waves.
- Electrical Engineers and Electronic Engineers may design electrical, computer and automation systems, alarms, and communication systems. They may also develop the technology to generate, store, or distribute the renewable energy harvested. They may be responsible for grid connections, designing the transmission lines and the offshore logistics of transporting energy underwater and back to land.
- Environmental Engineers may participate in the design to protect people and the environment by limiting toxic materials, they assess the processes used during construction and study the potential impact on marine life and the water.
- Marine Engineers may develop all of the support services necessary for the safety and comfort of installers, operators and/or maintenance technicians.
- Materials Engineers may research advanced materials that may be able to withstand corrosion, wave impacts, storms and the constant motion of the ocean while also lowering cost and improving the stability of the integrated systems.
- Mechanical Engineers may design specific items of machinery like cranes, hoists, elevators, and equipment for installing, anchoring, or moving structures and supplies. They may also manage the manufacturing processes for

the turbines, gearboxes, towers, and blades and other technology. They may also research ways to improve turbine aerodynamics while lowering the cost.

- Ocean Engineers with a Civil Engineering emphasis may design the OTEC and offshore wind turbine structures that are embedded in the ocean floor that can withstand hurricane winds. They may be responsible for mooring systems and running electrical cable underwater.

- Ocean Engineers with an Electrical Engineering emphasis may develop the technology to generate, store, or distribute the renewable energy harvested. They may be responsible for grid connections, designing the transmission lines and the offshore logistics of transporting energy underwater and back to land.

- Ocean Engineers with a Mechanical Engineering emphasis may design energy and control systems that can withstand corrosion, wave impacts, storms and the constant motion of the ocean. They may build and test prototypes, make CAD models, or write and apply for patents.

Hydropower Energy Engineering

Walk up to your kitchen sink and turn on the water full blast. Stick your hand under the stream of water with your palm facing up. You should feel the water pushing your hand down. Depending on your water system, the water flows at around 1 gallon per minute. You have to use a little muscle to hold your hand under the stream. Now imagine millions of gallons of water crashing into your palm. Engineers have figured out how to harness power like that, and it's called hydropower.

Hydropower, or hydroelectric power, is the most common and least expensive source of renewable electricity in the United States today. Hydropower has been in use for many years because it is readily available, clean (has no emissions), and is endlessly renewable. It is mainly used in the Pacific Northwest, and according to the Energy Information Administration, there are more than 160 hydroelectric facilities in the region. These facilities provided more than 6% of the country's electricity in 2008, and about 70% of all renewable electricity generated in the United States came from hydropower resources.

Although hydropower is clean and abundant, the downside is that the dams needed can adversely affect the surrounding region and wildlife populations. In the Pacific Northwest, salmon populations need to swim upriver to lay their eggs, so a hydroelectric dam that blocks their path could have disastrous effects. Wild salmon rivers are core centers of abundance and diversity, serving as the foundation for healthy wild fisheries, ecosystems, economies, and communities. To solve this problem, engineers have created fish ladders that allow the salmon and other fish to continue their journey upstream without harm. Another solution that engineers are investigating is the ability to build a hydroelectric facility without the need to create a dam at all!

There are two main types of hydropower plants:

1. Large-Scale—
   These plants
   were developed
   to produce
   electricity for
   government or
   electric utility
   projects. They
   produce the
   most electricity

Bonneville Dam in Oregon

by using a dam and a reservoir to hold water from a river. When electricity is needed, the water is released. The rushing water turns a turbine that generates electricity.

When the electricity is in low demand, these hydropower plants can also act as power storage facilities by reversing the process and pumping water back into the upper reservoir to be stored until more electricity is needed.

2. Microhydro—These plants were developed to produce electricity (low-voltage power) for smaller energy needs such as those of farms, ranches, homes, and villages. They also use the energy of flowing water to produce electricity. A river will flow downhill. For microhydro projects, a portion of the water is diverted to a canal or pipeline that runs through a powerhouse that contains a turbine or waterwheel. Waterwheels are no longer practical but may still exist in many powerhouses. Powerhouses generate electricity by converting the mechanical energy of turning turbine blades into electricity. The water that turned the turbine or waterwheel is then returned to the river, and power lines take the electricity to a house along the river.

ENGINEERS THAT HELP HARVEST HYDROPOWER

•   Civil Engineers design and direct the construction of dams to prevent flooding, improve irrigation, provide a water supply, and generate hydroelectric power. Civil engineering is closely connected to the environment, both natural and human-made.

•   Construction Engineers are concerned with the planning and management of the construction of the dam. Construction of such projects requires knowledge of engineering, management principles, business procedures, economics, and human behavior. Construction engineers engage in the design of temporary structures, as well as cost estimating, planning and scheduling, and cost control.

- Dredging Engineers ensure that a river is always kept at the appropriate depth and width so ships and other watercraft can move safely and easily. They may improve the waterways by building breakwaters and jetties to protect homes and businesses from crashing waves. They often remove the sediments from the waterways and use it for other beneficial purposes such as creating islands and wetlands or improving habitats.

- Electrical Engineers ensure the thousands of gigawatt-hours of electricity created by the dam are delivered to the right place. Some electrical engineers design and build devices that increase the efficiency of the energy generated. Almost anything that uses electricity from the smallest battery, a wall plug, or an ultra-high voltage transmission line, relies to some extent on the work of an electrical engineer.

- Geological Engineers and geotechnical engineers help find the best ways to use the earth's resources to solve technical problems without damaging the environment. Geologic engineers study the rocks and ground of a dam site, understand how to reduce flooding and landslides and solve problems associated with building the dam and power plant in the middle of a river.

- Hydropower Engineers make hydropower facilities more efficient at capturing energy and make dams more environmentally friendly. Hydropower planning falls under the larger umbrella of water resource engineering, so hydropower engineers are typically civil engineers who have knowledge of hydropower and water resource management and planning.

- Mechanical Engineers create, design, construct, and install of many of the mechanical devices of the dam and lock such as the turbines, generators, and power distribution systems.

- Power Engineers combine electrical, chemical, structural, and mechanical engineering. Generating electricity is more than turning on a switch—a lot more. It includes not only generating power but also transmitting and distributing it.

Geothermal Energy Engineering

One of the best demonstrations of the power of geothermal energy is Old Faithful, a geothermal geyser in Yellowstone National Park. In general, the temperature of the upper ten feet of ground under your feet is between 45-75 degrees all year round. Of course, the temperature of the top few feet change with the seasons. On a very hot and sunny day, that few feet may be very warm and on a cold winter day, it may be very cold; but once you dig below the surface, you will find that the temperature is 45-75 degrees.

As you dig deeper in the ground, the temperature gets warmer and warmer until it reaches 9000 degrees F at the Earth's core. Hot magma continuously flows through the core, heating underwater reservoirs to several hundreds of degrees. Geysers such as Old Faithful have surface vents for the hydrothermal explosions that occur far below the surface. A hydrothermal explosion occurs when water travels down a vent and comes into contact with the hot rocks and magma that are 6600 feet below the surface. This boils and pressurizes the water in such a way that it shoots out of the surface vent and sprays steam.

Geothermal energy may be one of the best sources available for renewable energy. Not only does it provide clean, sustainable heat from the earth, there is enough underground water available to supply our energy needs for 100,000 years according to the Geothermal Energy Association. A geothermal power plant creates no emissions and burns no fuel.

Currently geothermal power only supplies about 0.1% of our global energy needs. The reason more countries and areas of the United States don't use geothermal energy is that a power plant must be close to a tectonic plate where there is plenty of seismic activity. In other words, areas that often have earthquakes will have the hottest underground reservoirs. In the United Sates, California is famous for it's earthquakes so it is not surprising that it also has the largest geothermal field now operating in the world with 22 power plants supplying 5% of California's energy needs.

According to the Union of Concerned Scientists, there is 50,000 times more energy in the heat 33,000 fcct below the earth's surface than in all the oil and natural gas resources in the world. The challenge for engineers is getting to the extremely high temperature reservoirs and molten rock called within the earth's core.

To harvest electricity from a reservoir first requires that the reservoir water be very hot (225-600 degrees F). In the United States, although geothermal heat pumps can be found almost anywhere, geothermal power plants are located in the western states because the underground water temperature is the highest. These western power plants have been generating electricity for residential and commercial use since 1960. It is expected that as engineers research and develop the technology, this form of green energy will become much more cost effective and competitive with fossil fuels.

According to the Department of Energy, there are currently three types of geothermal power plants:
1. Dry Steam—Dry steam plants use steam from underground wells to rotate a turbine, which activates a generator to produce electricity. There are only two known underground resources of steam in the United States: The Geysers in northern California and Old Faithful in Yellowstone National Park in Montana. Because Yellowstone is protected from development, the power plants at The Geysers are the only dry steam plants in the country.

2. Flash Steam—The most common type of geothermal power plant, flash steam plants use water at temperatures of more than 360 degrees F. As this hot water flows up through wells in the ground, the decrease in pressure causes some of the water to boil. The steam created is then used to power a generator, and any leftover water and condensed steam is returned to the reservoir.

3. Binary Cycle—Binary cycle plants use the heat from lower-temperature reservoirs (225-360 degrees F) to boil a working fluid, which is then vaporized in a heat exchanger and used to power a generator. The water, which never comes into direct contact with the working fluid, is then injected back into the ground to be reheated.

In other parts of the United States and the world, geothermal heat pumps are used for residential and commercial buildings. There are over one million ground-source heat pumps installed in the US, and these can be installed right on a home or business owner's property to heat and cool the home or building. These heat pumps are much more efficient than normal heating and cooling systems. In fact, according to the EPA, they reduce electricity consumption by 30-60 percent and emit no pollution.

A geothermal heat pump (GHP) has three main elements:
1. A heat pump,
2. an air delivery system (ductwork), and
3. a heat exchanger (a system of pipes buried in shallow ground).

In the winter, the heat pump removes heat from the heat exchanger and pumps it into the indoor air delivery system. In the summer the process is reversed, and the heat pump moves heat from the indoor air into the heat exchanger. The heat removed from the indoor air during the summer can also be used to provide a free source of hot water.

There are many different types of geothermal heat pumps for different climates, soil conditions, available land, and applications. Along with heating and cooling homes, these heat pumps are also used to heat fish farms, greenhouses, and for pasteurizing milk.

With 50,000-60,000 new installations in homes, businesses, and schools every year, this industry is growing fast. Engineers are needed to develop new technologies for drilling deeper to capture the heat from "dry" rocks in other parts of the US. Because of the viability of geothermal energy, there is high demand for these types of engineers and technicians.

THE ENGINEERS WHO HELP HARVEST GEOTHERMAL ENERGY

- Civil and Structural Engineers specify the actual structure of the power plant.
- Civil or Mechanical Engineers with an emphasis in hydraulics manage the drilling process.
- Electrical Engineers and Electronic Engineers design electrical, computer, and automation systems, alarms, and communication systems. They may also develop the technology to generate, store, or distribute the renewable energy harvested.
- Environmental Engineers participate in the design and drilling processes to protect people and the environment by limiting toxic materials. They assess the processes used during construction and study the potential impact on the environment. They may also prepare environmental impact studies for regulatory agencies.
- Geological Engineers identify underground reservoirs and suggest drilling equipment and techniques based on soil

and rock conditions. They may also prepare contour and other maps for forecasting drilling sites.

- Heating Ventilating and Air-Conditioning (HVAC) Engineers design, evaluate, and maintain GHPs. They may also be known as GHP HVAC engineers and are often mechanical engineers who have specialized in the thermal energy areas of mechanical engineering.
- Mechanical Engineers design, manufacture, and install GHP systems. They may also manage the manufacturing processes for the pipes, generators, motors, electrical components, and other technologies. In addition, they may also research ways to improve drilling or harvesting techniques while lowering the cost of the energy system.

Bioenergy Engineering

Although every industry needs environmentally conscious engineers, an excellent place to make a big difference is in bioenergy because bioenergy needs help. Considered by many as not purely green, it's a step in the right direction.

With fewer and fewer fossil fuels available, researchers turned to biomass as a way to fuel our cars and power our homes. Biomass is organic matter such as plants (switchgrass, barley, corn, and soybeans), trees (sweetgum, poplar and willow), residue from agriculture and forestry, animal fats, aquatic crops (algae, giant kelp, other seaweed, and marine microflora), and the organic component of municipal and industrial wastes (lumber and paper mill wasters also known as biomass feedstock). Because biomass refers to producing something from living matter, a simple form of this energy is getting heat from a wood fire. You are using organic matter (a tree) to produce energy (heat).

When we use biomass to produce electricity, this is known as biopower. According to the Department of Energy, biopower technologies include:

- Direct combustion—Most electricity generated from biomass is produced by direct combustion using conventional boilers. These boilers primarily burn waste wood products from the agriculture and wood-processing industries. When burned, the wood produces steam, which spins a turbine. The spinning turbine then activates a generator that produces electricity.
- Co-firing—Co-firing involves replacing a portion of the fuel in coal-fired boilers with biomass. Co-firing has been successfully demonstrated in most boiler technologies. Co-firing biomass can significantly reduce the sulfur dioxide emissions of coal-fired power plants, and is the cheapest renewable energy option for many power producers.
- Anaerobic digestion—Anaerobic digestion, or methane recovery, is a common technology used to convert organic waste to electricity or heat. In anaerobic digestion, organic matter is decomposed by bacteria in the absence of oxygen to produce methane and other by-products that form a renewable natural gas. It can be made from recycled cooking oil and other oil sources.

One of the problems with biomass is the resources that it uses to produce energy. It takes land and water to grow plants. Plants grown for fuel take up space that could be used to grow food and burning this biomass release greenhouse gases into the atmosphere. If food becomes a scarce resource, the prices will rise making it harder for struggling families to put food on the table. In addition, according to Smithsonian magazine, it would require 2 billion acres of corn per year to provide enough ethanol for the 200 million cars in America. The potential farmland in the United States is only 800 million acres, which is less than half of the 2 billion. This does leave room for new products to be developed from plants that are not food stock. Research has been ongoing for the use of kudzu, a very invasive vine that grows wild all over the south, for making fuel. Leaves and grass clippings are another potential source that currently is considered waste.

To address these issues, engineers at the ORNL Bioenergy Feedstock Development Program (BFDP) has been developing and demonstrating environmentally acceptable crops and cropping systems for producing large quantities of low-cost, high-quality biomass which may be used to produce electricity and fuel our transportation. These crops take up less space, have better erosion control, and fewer fertilizer and pesticide requirements, and include switchgrass, the stems or stalks of alfalfa, and sorghum. BFDP also develops the technology and information needed to use agricultural, forestry, and urban residues for energy production.

According to the ORNL, "The energy absorbed by plants on land (and plankton in the seas) is recycled naturally through the process of life on Earth until it is eventually radiated away as low-temperature heat (except perhaps for a small Earth-bound fraction which may very slowly become fossil fuel). If we, the human race, intervene and "capture" some of the biomass at the stage where it is acting as a store of chemical energy, we have a renewable fuel. This has two major implications for the environment. Firstly, by burning biomass fuels we generate no more heat and create no more carbon dioxide than would have been produced in any case by natural processes. Secondly, provided our consumption of biomass does not exceed the natural level of recycling (which is very large), we have a renewable energy source whose use does not substantially disturb the natural biogeochemical cycle on a human time scale."

Possibly one of the best options for biomass on the horizon is algae. Algae can counter a lot of the problems with corn ethanol (high levels of corn ethanol production aren't sustainable). Algae can grow inexpensively in tanks on any land that has sunshine. It grows much faster than traditional farm crops, and the micro-organisms may even be able to use wastewater or salt water from the ocean, rather than fresh water.

In other words if this is interesting to you, it's a good time to think about an engineering career working with this renewable energy. The earth is a big place and can provide a lifetime of research and work in bioenergy discovery and exploration. As technologies develop to more efficiently process complex feedstocks, the biomass resource base will expand. The one thing we know for sure is that we need to stop burning fossil fuels and biomass can provide a very viable alternative.

THE ENGINEERS WHO HELP HARVEST BIOENERGY

- Agricultural Engineers may research environmentally acceptable crops and cropping systems for producing large quantities of low-cost, high-quality biomass or research crops that take up less crop space, have better erosion control, and fewer fertilizer and pesticide requirements.
- Electrical Engineers and Electronic Engineers design electrical, computer and automation systems, alarms, and communication systems. They may also develop the technology to generate, store, or distribute the renewable energy harvested.
- Environmental Engineers study the potential impact on the environment. They may also prepare environmental impact studies for regulatory agencies.

Chapter 2

Green Transportation

Green transportation is the future. The greatest possibility for a greener planet comes from the transportation sector which accounts for 67 percent of the US oil use and contributes one-third of the nation's greenhouse gas emissions. By developing technologies that conserve energy rather than importing the oil needed to create petroleum-based fuel, we reap two benefits: a significant increase in green jobs and increased health and environmental well-being.

If you want to work in this sector, the most useful things that you can do are:
1. Help reduce or eliminate emissions on vehicles.
2. Improve the miles per gallon or miles per charge of every vehicle or mode of transportation.
3. Develop new cleaner fuels and supporting technologies.
4. Make it easier for people to take mass transportation.
5. Develop easy to access electrical charging stations.

Moving towards greener transportation means that there will be plentiful opportunities for professionals who design, test, analyze, and improve the many components of new fuel-efficient, no emission or lower-emission cars, trucks, buses, trains, ships, and airplanes. Retrofitting and converting older vehicles to electric or alternative fuels is also a great opportunity to not only help improve the environment, but also to preserve a piece of our history. Work in this green sector means lots of jobs for mechanical engineers but many other types of engineers such as, materials, aerospace, chemical, electrical, manufacturing, and computer will also benefit.

There is a need for professionals that can evaluate, design, and upgrade our current infrastructure and also a need for new or expanded transportation systems. The Federal Highway Administration approved over 6,000 projects in response to the American Recovery and Reinvestment Act of 2009. Improving infrastructure means more jobs for civil, environmental, geological, and structural engineers.

Automobiles

Because of environmental concerns and increased fuel-efficiency regulations and air-quality standards, this is a great time to become an automotive engineer. In fact, if motorized vehicles are your interest, there is no better career to pursue than engineering. There are more engineers in this sector than any other type of professional worker. Engineers are needed to design, test, and evaluate the safety and performance of every system within every type of vehicle. Electric cars, hybrids, and alternative-fuel vehicles all have teams of engineers behind the engines, transmissions, suspensions, brakes, electrical and computer systems, aerodynamics, and manufacturing processes.

Automotive engineering is a branch of mechanical engineering. According to the Department of Labor, by the year 2018, there will be an extra 87,000 jobs for mechanical engineers, and mechanical engineering is listed as one of the 50 occupations with the most openings that requires a bachelor's degree. Most students interested in this type of career major in mechanical engineering with an emphasis in automotive engineering. Because mechanical engineering is such a broad discipline, select a school whose area of emphasis matches your own interests. If you are interested in automotive engineering, select a college that teaches mechanical engineering with an emphasis in automotive engineering such as the Universities of Illinois, Michigan, or Tennessee. If your primary interest is to make cars or any vehicle go faster, choose a school with an emphasis in combustion, materials, fluid mechanics, or thermodynamics. If electric cars are your interest, choose a school that specializes or has classes in battery technology.

Of course if you don't know which of these specialty areas interest you the most, a good, broad-based mechanical engineering degree will give you many options. You can learn specialties after you've worked in the industry and taken classes for specific certifications. Professional engineering licenses always require continuing education and classes can be used to both maintain your license and help with your specialty.

Most automotive engineers are employed by major automobile companies, but they may also work for bus manufacturers, aviation companies, off road vehicle companies, motorcycle companies, among others. In the US there are almost 10,000 companies that design and manufacture car parts, and with new types of vehicles on the horizon, this number is expected to increase. From researching alternative fuels and aerodynamics to increase the fuel efficiency of vehicles to improving the suspensions of sports cars or electric buses, these engineers are leading the way to lower emissions and a healthier planet.

Thanks to the competitiveness of the automotive industry, these engineers can expect a future of growth in an exciting and challenging environment. Car makers are clamoring for engineers to help them meet new governmental regulations and develop cars that an environmentally conscious public wants to purchase. Automotive engineers enjoy benefits such as experiencing cutting-edge technology first hand, being involved in several stages of new car development, and receiving discounts on their own new vehicles.

Honda and Ford Motor Company both offer internship and co-op work experience for students interested in automotive engineering. Ford offers hands-on experience working full time during the summer, and Honda offers year round internships, part-time jobs (2 days a week), and co-op programs.

Toyota employs 317,000 people worldwide and seeks graduates that have a B.S. in mechanical engineering. They also look for people with a general understanding of engineering theory, excellent problem solving techniques, an understanding and willingness to work on CAD systems. As with other engineering disciplines, you will also need excellent communication and interpersonal skills, and experience in an automotive internship or co-op (which are good qualities for working for any transportation company).

According to the New York Times, GM, Ford, and Chrysler will need to hire thousands of engineers to meet the demand for cars that get 54.5 miles per gallon (mpg) by the year 2026 set by the Obama Administration. Car manufacturers understand that being green is not only good for the environment but it's also critical to being competitive worldwide. As the general population becomes more educated about the importance of fuel efficiency, they are demanding car manufacturers produce vehicles that meet higher fuel standards. Auto makers are currently working with colleges and universities to develop courses to train and retrain the engineers who will develop tomorrow's electric, hybrid, and alternative-fuel cars. Karl Stracke, GM's vice president of global vehicle engineering, said today's automotive engineers must be cross-trained in several different types of engineering to make the vehicles we need and compete in the future global market.

ELECTRIC VEHICLES

Electric cars are already available and will play a larger role in our future. They are environmentally friendly alternatives to combustion engine (gas or diesel) cars because they create no tail pipe emissions. In these cars, the gas or diesel motor is replaced by an electric motor that is powered by rechargeable batteries. Tremendous research and experimentation is being undertaken by engineers to find a way to extend battery life so that people can travel further on a single charge. Most electric vehicles have a range of less than 100 miles, but as technology is developed you can expect that engineers will find a way to solve this problem. Just look at the fully electric Tesla Roadster that can go 245 miles on a charge and from 0 to 60 mph in 4 seconds. The price tag is prohibitive for most of the public but the technology has been created. It's now all about refining the technology to bring the cost down.

If working in the electric car industry sounds exciting, this may be a great time because not only are there many jobs for engineers designing the cars themselves, there are also jobs creating the infrastructure needed to support the electric car industry. For example, engineers are needed to design charging stations along interstates and near businesses. Some of these may be wired to the grid or may be solar powered. San Francisco and other large metropolitan areas have rewritten their building codes to mandate that  every new building include wiring for car charging stations. Engineers also recently developed piezoelectric crystals (crystals that produce electricity when pressure is applied) that can be inserted in roadbeds so that as the cars drive over them the crystals recharge the car battery thereby extending the range of electric cars. There is tremendous opportunity for engineers in the electric car industry.

Although electric vehicles will soon be the standard, there are some downsides to this alternative. Batteries to fuel these vehicles contain highly toxic materials and can present an extensive problem for engineers. To resolve this issue, engineers are creating better systems for reusing and recycling. Another downside is charging batteries. Unless the homeowner has a solar charging station, these cars will be charged on our nation's power grid which is aging and also uses fossil fuels.

HYBRID VEHICLES

Hybrid electric vehicles (HEVs) are cars or other vehicles that combine an internal-combustion engine powered by gasoline, diesel, compressed natural gas, hydrogen, or other fuels, with one or more electric motors powered by a energy-storage device such as a battery or ultracapacitor. So HEVs are a cross between traditional engine vehicles and electric vehicles.

While electric car systems are being perfected, HEVs are a great alternative because they combine the benefits of high-fuel economy and low emissions with the power, range, and convenience of conventional engines. According to the Alternative Fuels and Advanced Vehicles Data Center, HEV vehicles may one day be 2–3 times more efficient than conventional vehicles.

HEV technologies also have potential to be combined with flex fuels and fuel cells to provide additional benefits. Many HEV owners enjoy the fact that the battery is recharged while they drive so the vehicle never needs to be plugged in. The most popular example of this type of vehicle is the Toyota Prius.

PLUG-IN HYBRID ELECTRIC VEHICLES

A plug-in hybrid electric vehicle (PHEV) is similar to an HEV except that you can also recharge the battery by plugging the car into an electricity source. In fact, PHEV batteries can be charged by an outside electric power source, by the internal combustion engine, or through regenerative braking. During braking the electric motor acts as a generator, using the energy to charge the battery.

PHEVs have a larger battery pack than HEVs that increases the "all electric range" of the vehicle. PHEVs can typically travel 10–40 miles on only electricity.

Another advantage of the PHEV over the HEV is that the HEV typically uses battery power when traveling under 40 mph and the combustion engine (which recharges the battery) when traveling faster than 40 mph. If you are driving primarily in the city at speeds under 40 mph, a HEV battery may go dead or switch to using its combustion engine, and you would lose the valuable benefits of having a low-emissions vehicle. In addition, using electricity from the grid to run the vehicle some of the time costs less and reduces petroleum consumption compared with conventional vehicles. PHEVs might also reduce emissions, depending on the electricity source. It is possible for a PHEV owner to get to and from work on all-electric power, plug in the vehicle to charge it at night, and be ready for another all-electric commute the next day.

The first mass produced PHEV available in the US is the Chevy Volt. Currently PHEVs are typically more expensive than similar conventional and hybrid vehicles, but some of the cost can be recovered through fuel savings, a federal tax credit, and state incentives.

BIOFUELS

In the last chapter, we discussed the ways that we could use biomass to create electricity. In this chapter, we continue the discussion because biomass is also used to produce fuel for transportation.

Biofuels are liquid or gaseous fuels produced from biomass. The expanded use of biofuels offers an array of benefits for our energy security, economic growth, and environment.

Current biofuels research focuses on new forms of biofuels such as:

1. Ethanol—an alcohol, is a high-octane fuel that is made primarily from the starch in corn grain and works well in internal combustion engines (Octane helps prevent

engine knocking and is extremely important in engines designed to operate at a higher compression ratio, so they generate more power.) In fact, Henry Ford and other early automakers thought ethanol would be the world's primary fuel before gasoline became so readily available. Ford worked with George Washington Carver, the scientist and inventor from Tuskegee Institute, who found multiple uses for peanuts and other crops. Ford thought the ethanol produced would be ideal. It is most commonly used as an additive to petroleum-based fuels to reduce toxic air emissions and increase octane. Today, roughly half of the gasoline sold in the United States includes 5–10 percent ethanol. Studies have estimated that ethanol and other biofuels could replace 30 percent or more of US gasoline demand by 2030. Low-level blends of ethanol, such as E10 (10 percent ethanol, 90 percent gasoline) generally have a higher octane rating than unleaded gasoline. Low-octane gasoline can be blended with 10 percent ethanol to attain the standard 87-octane requirement.

Several steps are required to make ethanol available as a vehicle fuel. Biomass feedstocks are grown and transported to ethanol production facilities. After ethanol is produced at the facilities, a distribution network supplies ethanol-gasoline blends to fueling stations for use by drivers.

2. Biodiesel use is relatively small, but its benefits to air quality are dramatic. Biodiesel is less toxic, biodegradable, and burns cleaner than petroleum-based diesel fuel. When cars with diesel engines pull into a fueling station, they will see B20, which is 20 percent biodiesel and 80 percent petroleum diesel. This is the most common biodiesel blend in the United States. Biodiesel is a great alternative because it is a domestically produced renewable fuel that can be manufactured from vegetable oils, animal fats, or recycled restaurant greases.

3. Algae—Many algae strains contain over 50 percent oil, which can easily be converted to biodiesel fuel. The algae energy source offers various advantages that other sources of renewable energy don't have. For example, soybeans and corn are frequently used in biofuel production, but developing countries are fiercely against this, because these crops are not being used for food, and they are taking up fertile land, which is becoming scarce around the world. Algae can grow inexpensively in tanks on any land that has sunshine. It grows much faster than traditional farm crops, and the micro-organisms may even be able to use wastewater (water not suitable for farming or drinking) or salt water from the ocean, rather than fresh water. An additional benefit is that because algae is a plant, it will not only clean the water but also clean the atmosphere by capturing carbon dioxide, one of the harmful greenhouse gases.

FLEX FUEL

A Flexible Fuel Vehicle (FFV) has an engine that is similar to a standard conventional engine. FFVs look like any other conventional vehicle and have the same power, towing capacity, acceleration, and cruise speed as conventional vehicles. The difference is that they can use a gasoline fuel mixture that contains ethanol for lower emissions. However, the downside is the miles per gallon are lower when the FFV runs on E85 (higher ethanol mixture) than when it runs on E10 (lower ethanol mixture) gasoline but E85 is typically less expensive so the cost per mile is comparable to powering a gasoline car.

E85 (85 percent ethanol, 15 percent gasoline) is considered a flexible fuel and requires an engine that is made up of ethanol-compatible components and set to accommodate the higher oxygen content of E85. E85 should only be used in ethanol-capable FFVs (in fact, it's illegal to use E85 in a non-FFV).

E10 (10 percent ethanol, 90 percent gasoline) is the standard gasoline in many states and is classified as "substantially similar" to gasoline by the Environmental Protection Agency. This means they can be used legally in any gasoline-powered vehicle.

The 15 percent gasoline content in E85 enables flexible fuel vehicles to operate normally under cold conditions, but fueling a vehicle with pure ethanol (E100) creates problems during cold-weather operation.

FFVs qualify as Alternative Fuel Vehicles (AFVs) under the Energy Policy Act of 1992 (EPAct). They also qualify for AFV tax credits.

FUEL CELLS AND HYDROGEN VEHICLES

If you live in an area that is overcast all the time and never windy, instead of using wind turbines or solar panels, you could use hydrogen. Hydrogen can be made using renewable energy sources, stored, and shipped anywhere in the world to power a fuel cell—providing a truly renewable source of energy to any location.

Elements, like hydrogen, are the building blocks of the universe. Hydrogen was first classified as a distinct element by Henry Cavendish in 1766. It is known as Element 1 because it has one electron and one proton, making it the first element listed in the periodic table.

Hydrogen is the smallest and lightest element in the universe, and it is the most abundant. The word hydrogen comes from the Greek words hydro, which means "water," and genes, meaning "forming." It is estimated that hydrogen makes up more than 90 percent of the total molecules in the observable universe. Of all the elements, hydrogen has the highest energy content per unit of weight.

How a PEM Fuel Cell Works

A Proton Exchange Membrane (PEM) fuel cell converts the chemical energy of hydrogen and oxygen into electrical energy. The fuel cell itself has no moving parts. The heart of a PEM fuel cell is a polymer (perflorinated sulfonic acid polymer) called a proton exchange membrane (also known as polymer electrolyte membrane) that acts as an electrolyte.

Platinum is attached to the fuel cell's membrane as a catalyst. When a hydrogen molecule with one negative electron and one positive proton is introduced to the membrane, the platinum along with the membrane creates an environment that allows the positive proton to pass through the membrane, but the negative electron does not pass through.

The electrons begin to move along a path, creating electricity that is captured as the electron moves through a current collector to the other side of the fuel cell. The electron rejoins a proton, and the newly formed hydrogen atoms join oxygen to produce water. This reaction also generates heat. Therefore, the output of a hydrogen PEM fuel cell includes electricity, heat and pure, clean water.

Electrolysis is the process of converting electrical energy into chemical potential energy. In the 1780s, scientist Antonie Lavoisier discovered a way to split water molecules into hydrogen and oxygen and then recombine them to make water again. When an electrical charge is applied to water, the charge breaks the chemical bond between the hydrogen and oxygen and splits apart the atomic components creating charged particles called ions.

An electrolyzer has two electrodes where the ions form. One electrode, called the anode, is positively charged. The other electrode, called the cathode, is negatively charged.

Hydrogen gathers at the negative cathode, and the positively charged anode attracts oxygen. A voltage of about 1.6 V is required for electrolysis to take place. This voltage requirement increases or decreases with changes in temperature and pressure. Adding an electrolyte such as salt to water increases the rate at which hydrogen and oxygen are produced.

Reversible fuel cells can be used to perform electrolysis. In a fuel cell, the electrolyte is a polymer that looks like clear plastic and is part of the fuel cell membrane assembly. When you apply current to a fuel cell, it will electrolyze water, giving you hydrogen on the cathode side and oxygen on the anode side.

Fuel cells generate electricity from a simple electrochemical reaction in which oxygen and hydrogen combine to form water. There are several different types of fuel cells but they are all based around a central design that consists of two electrodes, a negative anode, and a positive cathode. These are separated by a solid or liquid electrolyte that carries electrically charged particles between the two electrodes. A catalyst, such as platinum, is often used to speed up the reactions at the electrodes.

The history of the fuel cell began in the early 1960s. A new US government agency, NASA, was looking for a way to power a series of upcoming manned space flights. NASA had already ruled out using batteries because they were too heavy, solar energy because it was too expensive, and nuclear power because it was too risky. The fuel cell was looked upon as a possible solution, and NASA awarded a number of research contracts to develop a practical working design.

This search led to the development of the first proton exchange membrane. A chemist working for General Electric (GE) further modified the original fuel cell design by using a sulphonated polystyrene ion-exchange membrane as the electrolyte. Three years later another GE chemist devised a way of depositing platinum on to this membrane, and this became known as the Grubb-Niedrach fuel cell. GE went on to develop this technology with NASA and it was used on the Gemini space project.

While this versatile option holds much promise, there are still many environmental and sustainability issues to resolve. Expensive and toxic platinum is currently required for the fuel cell reaction. Additionally, power density is relatively low compared to today's standards and there are issues surrounding the safety of storing hydrogen. Nevertheless, giant strides are being made in every facet of the technology with billions of dollars flowing into research and development in both the private and public sector.

THE ENGINEERS WHO HELP PRODUCE GREENER AUTOMOBILES

- Automotive Engineers may design, test, and evaluate the safety and performance of every system within every type of vehicle. Electric cars, hybrids, and alternative fuel vehicles all have teams of engineers behind the engines, transmissions, suspensions, brakes, electrical and computer systems, aerodynamics, and manufacturing processes. There is no part of any vehicle that isn't designed, tested, analyzed, and evaluated by automotive engineers.
- Chemical, Agricultural, Environmental and Biological engineers all works in biofuels research and production.
- Computer and Electrical engineers may build the microprocessors that control the engine, or the anti-lock braking systems, emissions, smart locks, airbags, GPS, stereo, and fuel injection systems within a vehicle. They also create the systems that inform the owners of needed maintenance. They may also design the computerized equipment that allows mechanics to diagnose vehicle problems.
- Environmental engineers monitor and assess the environmental impact of green automobile manufacturing systems, fuels, batteries, paints and everything in betweeen.
- Mechanical Engineers decide on the size, shape, and materials of every part of every vehicle. They may be

involved in research, materials applications, safety features, alternative fuels, manufacturing, systems management, or any other facet of getting a vehicle onto the road. Mechanical engineering is the most popular major for students that want to get into the automotive industry.

- Manufacturing and Industrial Engineers evaluate, troubleshoot, validate, and improve manufacturing processes of vehicles, new technologies, and the equipment that produces vehicles. They are also responsible for all aspects of purchasing electronic and mechanical components and products.
- Materials and Chemical Engineers may research advanced materials that may be able to improve efficiency while also lowering the cost. They may also research new applications of technology such as integrating solar cells into windows or paint.

Mass Transit

One of the best ways to green the world is to increase the accessibility and availability of mass, or public transit. Mass transit can help alleviate congestion on our roadways and in our skies, increase  convenience for travelers, and reduce greenhouse gas emissions. Upgrading our rail system will also improve the efficiency of freight movement in America, which can eventually reduce the prices of goods and services.

According to *Green Jobs: a Guide to Eco Friendly Employment*, transporting goods by diesel railroad is already 8 times more energy efficient than carrying the same cargo by diesel trucks. Also, if the rail system was electric it would be twice as green. Even in a worst-case scenario, the system would emit two-thirds less carbon dioxide per mile than that powered by diesel fuel, and it would cost 5–6 times less. In the process, refurbishing and converting these systems would create a huge number of American jobs.

According to the August 2011 Transit Savings Report released by the American Public Transportation Authority (APTA), "individuals who switch from driving to riding public transportation can save, on average, up to $830 dollars this month, and up to $9,956 annually. These numbers show a substantial increase over this time last year, as gas prices have risen nearly $.86 a gallon." These savings are based on the August 10, 2011 average national gas price ($3.64 per gallon reported by AAA) and the national unreserved monthly parking rate of $155.22 per month.

"As gas prices remain high and the economy continues to flounder, Americans know they can rely on public transportation to provide a reliable, affordable way to get around," said APTA president William Millar. "Public transportation is now, and always has been a proven way to cut your transportation costs without limiting your ability to get where you need to go."

If you want to work in the mass transit sector as a green engineer, there are many paths you can follow. Buses can be electric, partially electric, or part of a system such as the Bus Rapid Transit (BRT) system. Subways, high-speed rail, and localized rapid transit systems all need passionate engineers to make mass transit more appealing, updated and accessible to the general public. We also need greener aircraft and ships that can carry thousands to millions of people across the oceans. There is tremendous variety for the engineer who is interested in green engineering and also mass transit.

BUSES, SUBWAYS AND RAIL SYSTEMS

The San Francisco Bay Area has BART (Bay Area Rapid Transit), Atlanta, Los Angeles, Miami, and Washington D.C. have the METRO, and many cities such as New York City have subways or some other type of rail systems. To get across the state or even the country, people can take Amtrak or buses. There are many ways for engineers to improve these systems and lessen their environmental impact.

When you think of greening buses, subways, and rail systems, there are three major ways that engineers are involved.
1. Engineers may work directly on the buses or rail cars making them more fuel efficient, powered by alternative energy, more aerodynamic, etc.
2. Engineers may work on the infrastructure of the transit systems to make them more appealing, efficient, accessible, and environmentally and user friendly.
3. Engineers may investigate locations to put it. They may investigate sites for transit systems that reduce harmful environmental impacts. These engineers understand laws and regulations concerning land easements and natural resource protection.
4. In addition to the paths that the trains and buses follow, engineers are needed to create the parking structures and transit stations, and must study and create a way of preserving habitats.
5. Engineers may work on smart traffic systems. By designing smart traffic systems, engineers help anticipate problems, alleviate congestion and decrease emergency-response times.

According the Reed Brockman, author of *From Sundaes to Space Stations: Careers in Civil Engineering,* "when you think of being a transportation engineer, think of yourself as part sculptor, part lawyer, and part environmentalist." As a transit engineer, you have the opportunity to make a substantial contribution to reduce economic strain, produce inspiring transit stations, and protect the environment.

THE ENGINEERS WHO HELP PRODUCE GREEN BUSES, SUBWAYS AND RAIL SYSTEMS

- Civil Engineers may design and build the infrastructure for the buses, subways, and rail systems.
- Computer and Electrical Engineers may build the computer systems that control the mass transit systems.
- Mechanical Engineers may design all the systems that not only control the transportation but also their design, manufacturing, and troubleshooting.
- Manufacturing and Industrial Engineers evaluate, troubleshoot, validate, and improve manufacturing processes of the green buses, subways ,and rail systems, new technologies, and the equipment that produces them. They are also responsible for all aspects of purchasing electronic and mechanical components and products.
- Materials and Chemical Engineers may research advanced materials for bullet trains that may be able to improve efficiency while also lowering the cost.
- Transportation Engineers alongside civil engineers are needed to design the infrastructure and paths for the subways, trains, and electric buses.

AIRCRAFT

Boeing's 787 Dreamliner is made of almost 50 percent carbon fiber, which is lighter and stronger than aluminum. The lighter material makes it a green aircraft because it uses 20 percent less fuel that airplanes of a similar size, and reduces emissions (emissions from one transatlantic flight can be as much as one automobile releases in 50 years of driving). This investment by

Boeing in new high-tech materials for their aircraft is a giant step toward cleaning our environment. Boeing is reaping its reward by investing in a green aircraft design—upon release, Boeing had sold out of this aircraft for the next three years.

About 60 percent of aviation emissions come from international flights, which are not covered by the Kyoto Protocol and its emissions reduction targets. In addition, because the emissions are released high in the atmosphere, they contribute to global climate change much faster than emissions released by cars and factories closer to the ground. According to the International Civil Aviation Organization's Carbon Emissions Calculator, a round trip flight for one person from San Francisco to Boston uses 30,592 Kg of fuel (10,538 gallons) and generates 694.76 Kg of carbon dioxide.

The environmental impact from aviation is increasing as more people travel by air and the number of planes built increases. Even though modern airplanes, jets, turboprops, and helicopters are more fuel efficient than 30 years ago, green engineering is still in very high demand to help design and produce:
- more fuel-efficient aircraft,
- improved aircraft technologies,
- alternative fuels, and
- to create improved ground airport vehicles, greener airport buildings, and airport infrastructure.

The aviation industry needs and hires all types of engineers to meet the demands of air travel.

Other alternative fuel pursuits have been:
- In December 2008, an Air New Zealand jet completed the world's first commercial aviation test flight partially using jatropha-based fuel. Jatropha, used for biodiesel, can thrive on marginal agricultural land where many trees and crops won't grow. Air New Zealand set several general sustainability criteria for its Jatropha, saying that such biofuels must not compete with food resources, that

they must be as good as traditional jet fuels, and that they should be cost competitive with existing fuels.

- In January 2009, Continental Airlines used a biofuel blend including components derived from algae and jatropha plants to power a commercial aircraft for the first time in North America. This demonstration flight marks the first sustainable biofuel demonstration flight by a commercial carrier using a twin-engined aircraft.

- One fuel biofuel alternative to aviation gasoline (avgas) that is under development to power piston-engine airplane motors is Swift Fuel (SF). Mary Rusek, president and co-owner of Swift Enterprises predicts that, "100SF will be comparably priced, environmentally friendlier and more fuel-efficient than other general aviation fuels on the market".

- In June 2011, revised international aviation fuel standards officially allow commercial airlines to blend conventional jet fuel with up to 50 percent biofuels.

- In December 2011, the FAA announced it is awarding $7.7 million to eight companies to advance the development of drop-in commercial aviation biofuels, with a special focus on ATJ (alcohol to jet) fuel. As part of its CAAFI (Commercial Aviation Alternative Fuel Initiative) and CLEEN (Continuous Lower Emissions, Energy and Noise) programs, the FAA plans to assist in the development of a sustainable fuel (from alcohols, sugars, biomass, and organic matter such as pyrolysis oils) that can be "dropped in" to aircrafts without changing current infrastructure. The grant will also be used to research how the fuels affect engine durability and quality control standards.

Aeronautical and aerospace engineers design and develop green technology for commercial aviation, national defense, and space exploration. They may help design and manufacture green military aircraft, missiles, and spacecraft. Within this field, they may specialize in the structure of the aircraft, aerodynamics, guidance and control, propulsion and design, manufacturing, or a certain type of aircraft. Commercial airliners, military aircraft, space shuttles, satellites, rockets, and helicopters are all within reach for talented aeronautical engineers, who may also be referred to as astronautical, aviation, or rocket engineers.

Aeronautical and aerospace engineers work on the hundreds of satellites that orbit the earth, and on the commercial and military aircraft that carry millions of passengers. Other

areas of focus include developing materials that can withstand extreme temperatures, investigating biological implications of astronauts in space, and reducing the effects of sonic booms on the environment.

In 2011, Google sponsored The Green Flight Challenge. The Challenge was to build an aircraft that can fly 200 miles in under two hours using the energy equivalent of a gallon of gasoline per passenger. That is about half of what planes use right per passenger. The first place prize of $1.35 million was awarded to team Pipistrel-USA.com of State College, Pa. The second place prize of $120,000 went to team eGenius, of Ramona, California.

THE ENGINEERS WHO HELP PRODUCE GREEN AIRCRAFT

- Aeronautical and Aerospace Engineers may specialize in the structure of the aircraft, aerodynamics, guidance and control, propulsion and design, manufacturing, or a certain type of aircraft.
- Civil and Structural Engineers may be involved in site selection and the construction for any airline

manufacturing plant as well as all the infrastructure needed to produce and assemble aircraft parts.

- Electrical and Computer Engineers may develop the technology and computer systems that control the aircraft. They may be responsible for the electrical, computer, and automation systems, alarms, and communication systems.

- Environmental Engineers may participate in the design, manufacturing, or installation of projects to protect people and the environment by evaluating and limiting toxic materials. They also monitor the processes and environmental impact of manufacturing.

- Industrial Engineers are needed to optimize airline timetables. These engineers may find themselves manipulating route networks and flight frequencies to reduce the number of empty seats, which makes the flight more efficient and optimizes airspace use.

- Manufacturing Engineers evaluate, troubleshoot, validate, and improve manufacturing processes of all aircraft, and any other parts or systems used to assemble, test, or install the pieces.

- Materials and Chemical Engineers research advanced materials that may improve fuel efficiency while also lowering cost and improving the stability of the integrated systems.

- Mechanical Engineers may design any part of the aircraft, or they may build and test prototypes, make CAD models, or write and apply for patents. They may also provide installation of systems, troubleshooting, or repairs.

Ships and Ocean-Going Vessels

According to The US Department of Transportation, a ship carrying cargo uses only 10–20 percent of the energy that would be used by trucks to carry the same cargo. An inland barge can move one ton of freight about 514 miles on one gallon of fuel, a train can move one ton of freight about 202 miles on one gallon of fuel, and a truck can move one ton of freight about 59 miles on a gallon of fuel. The downside is that carbon dioxide emissions from shipping is currently estimated at 4 to 5 percent of the global total, and estimated by the International Maritime Organization (IMO) to rise by up to 72 percent by 2020 if no action is taken.

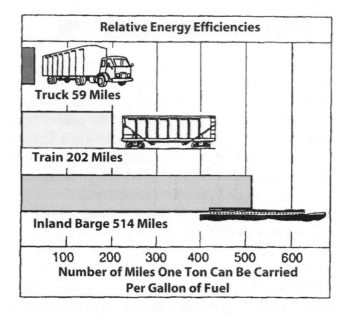

Marine engineering is a smaller field than mechanical or civil engineering, but the impact is far-reaching because 74 percent of the world's trade and 95 percent of US international trade is transported by ships.

Imagine the power required to move a 10,000 ton cargo ship through the water—maybe against the current—as it makes it way out to sea. As you can probably guess, the behemoth engines that do this job also use a tremendous amount of fuel and produce significant emissions. Fortunately, green engineers are already on the job looking for new ways to make ships more efficient and environmentally friendly. For example, SanSail, a green cargo ship company whose ships are powered by the wind and hydrogen fuels cells, is looking for ways to use wind turbines onboard cargo ships to "green" the transportation of wine along the California coast.

SanSail's strategy is to transport cargo whose value can be enhanced by ecologically sensitive delivery methods. SanSail will certify that products are delivered by the least environmentally harmful methods available. The technical strategy is to use a combination of minimally polluting technologies to offer consumers a choice of how their products are delivered as well as produced. The vessels will have zero operational carbon footprint.

Skysails, an engineering firm, is perfecting the world's first towing kite propulsion system for commercial shipping and luxury yachts. The sail looks like something you would use for parasailing except it is much bigger. When this kite is used to pull the ship, it can save 10 to 15 percent of the ship's fuel consumption. On a test voyage from Bremen to Venezuela, it is estimated that the fuel bill was cut by $1560 per day! That is good news for the environment, too!

The engineers that work in the maritime and ocean industries design anything that can be used as transportation on water, such as commercial, cargo, or Navy ships, yachts, submarines, seaplanes, and ice breaker ships. Maritime engineers also design underwater structures and ocean technology such as wind farms, diving gear, underwater robots (both remotely operated and autonomous), and underwater "cities" such as Aquarius, the underwater astronaut training center. Working in and near the ocean is unpredictable, corrosive, and sometimes hostile, so special training and systems are often required.

Marine structures, vehicles, and systems are unique and often expensive because they are large and complex, and only a few of each design are built. Anything that operates in or on the ocean has special design requirements for seakeeping, staying upright, capsizing, station-keeping, and enduring the random motions and loads of rogue waves and intense winds. Due to these unique requirements, manufacturing is often more challenging.

THE ENGINEERS WHO HELP PRODUCE GREEN SHIPS

- Civil Engineers specify the actual structure of the ship including framing, shell, decks, bulkheads, and equipment foundations. They ensure that the ship can withstand the weight of cargo and the impact of waves.
- Electrical Engineers provide for the generation and distribution of electricity throughout the ship for lighting, power, system controls, and various other ship services. Modern ships also require a multitude of electronic navigation, communication, and combat systems.
- Marine Engineers develop the propulsion plant, power plant, and all support services necessary for the safety and comfort of people onboard.
- Materials Engineers identify appropriate metals, plastics, paint, lubricants, equipment, cable, furniture, and other goods necessary to meet performance requirements over the lifetime of the ship, and work with manufacturers to ensure that materials that are purchased perform as specified.
- Mechanical Engineers design specific items of machinery like cranes, hoists, elevators, and equipment for anchoring, steering, controlling submarine depth, or moving weapons and other supplies within the ship, as well as between ships, at sea. Knowledge of fluid systems is required for designing fuel, lubrication, and water installations, as well as fire fighting, compressed air, and heating, ventilation, and air conditioning systems.
- Naval Engineers are responsible for the ship floating, maintaining an upright position when damaged, being steerable and steering straight, holding together in hundred-year storms, having motions that are tolerable to human beings and onboard equipment, surviving ice storms that encrust the vessel with heavy topside weights, protecting cargo and people from fires and explosions; all while allowing efficient operations at sea and pier-side with required maintenance and repair.

- Ocean Engineers concern themselves with work both on and below the surface of the sea, and study ocean movements and their affect on ships and craft both on the surface and below it. An ocean engineer may design small subsurface vehicles that perform ocean bottom scanning, salvage operations, object recovery, and submarine rescue. The work includes structural, propulsion, and hull-form design for resisting deep ocean pressure, and the selection of materials for this hostile environment.

Chapter Three

Green Construction

"My favorite part of the job is helping someone understand that being green can improve their life and save them money."
-Gay Taylor, PE, LEED AP BD+C, President, The Taylor Waller Companies and former Engineering Manager for Federal Express

Do you think a building can give you more energy, make you more alert, or healthier? Although the buildings we visit and the homes we live in protect us from sun, snow, rain, wind, and the other elements of nature, they also affect our health and the environment in many ways. If you have ever been in a green building, you have probably found that as well as being very comfortable, it was also beautiful. There was probably special care taken to have good indoor air quality, comfortable lighting, and be environmentally sustainable. That's part of what green building is all about. Green buildings can be homes, warehouses, skyscrapers, or any built structure that are designed to be sensitive to human health and the natural environment.

The energy used to heat and power non-green constructed buildings in the US produces 38.1 percent of the nation's total carbon dioxide emissions, consumes 12 percent of the total water used, and 39 percent of the total energy used. In addition, greenhouse gas emissions are also created from manufacturing new building materials and the debris from traditional construction fill landfills. Green construction addresses these issues by designing buildings that meet low emissions requirements and that have a higher rate of reuse and recycling at the end of its useful life.

There are many benefits to green construction. Not only is it good for the environment (green buildings can enhance and protect biodiversity, improving air and water quality, reduce waste, and conserve natural resources), but green buildings can also reduce operating costs and improve worker health and productivity.

GREEN BUILDING

Imagine that you are an engineer in charge of building a "green" high-rise for a large company in downtown San Francisco. What kinds of things must you consider?

You should start with the definition of a green building. Green building is the practice of creating structures and using processes that are environmentally responsible and resource-efficient throughout a building's lifecycle from siting to design, construction, operation, maintenance, renovation, and deconstruction. This practice expands and complements the classical building design concerns of economy, utility, durability, and comfort. A green building is also known as a sustainable or high-performance building.

A green building:
- Consumes less energy, water, materials, and natural resources.
- Protects people's health and sense of well-being.
- Reduces waste and pollution, and improves the environment.

For example, green buildings may incorporate sustainable

materials in their construction (such as reused, recycled-content, or those made from renewable resources); create healthy indoor environments with minimal pollutants; and feature landscaping and plumbing systems that reduces water usage (by collecting rainwater for many building and landscape requirements.)

Homes, schools, large buildings, laboratories and healthcare facilities all have the potential to become a green or sustainable buildings; however, every building type has different design and efficiency needs depending on its function. New buildings may be designed, built, and operated to be green buildings. Existing building can also become green through remodeling, retrofitting, and improving operations.

If you are a green engineer and want to work on making homes with less environmental impact (greener), you could reduce the need for artificial light, create a vegetated green roof to control storm water and decrease urban heat island effect, install low-flow plumbing fixtures to decrease water use, and use high recycled content materials in construction and furnishing.

Engineers in this sector design things such as:
- Water efficient toilets and faucets—Toilets are the main source of water use in the home by far, accounting for nearly 30 percent of residential indoor water consumption. Toilets are also a major source of wasted water due to leaks and inefficiency. WaterSense labeled toilets could save nearly 2 billion gallons of water per day across the country. Switching to high-efficiency toilets can save a family of four an average, $2,000 in water bills over the lifetime of the toilets. Faucets account for more than 15 percent of indoor household water use, which is more than 1 trillion gallons of water across the US each year. WaterSense labeled bathroom sink faucets and accessories can reduce a sink's water flow by 30 percent or more without sacrificing performance. If every household in the United States installed WaterSense faucets, we could save more than $350 million in water utility bills

and more than 60 billion gallons of water annually!

- High-efficiency showerheads—Showering accounts for about 17 percent of residential indoor water use in the US, which is more than 1.2 trillion gallons of water consumed each year. High-efficiency shower heads can save 25–60 percent of the water used with a traditional showerhead.

- Formaldehyde-free adhesives and finishes—Many bathroom cabinets are made from particle board, hardwood plywood paneling, or medium density fiberboard glued together using a formaldehyde-based adhesive. Formaldehyde is a common type of Volatile Organic Compound (VOC), a harmful chemical that can contribute to outdoor smog, as well as indoor air pollution. Finishes commonly used on cabinets also contain VOCs. VOC-free adhesives and finishes are mainly the work of chemical and materials engineers.

- Recycled-content materials and sustainably harvested furnishings and flooring—Engineers in the recycling industry are always on the lookout for ways to help ensure that materials collected in recycling programs are used again in the manufacture of new products. Green engineers can offer builders purchasing options by locating sustainably harvested woods and products that have low energy requirements in manufacturing and a low adverse environmental impact throughout the product's lifecycle. In addition, these recycled products usually contain fewer toxins or hazardous constituents such as VOCs, including those that can result in indoor air quality issues.

- Low-energy ventilation, and energy efficient heating and cooling systems—Too much moisture in a home can lead to mold, mildew, and other growths. This in turn can lead to a variety of health affects ranging from allergic reactions and asthma attacks to more serious illnesses. In addition to health problems, severe moisture problems can lead to rot, structural damage, or premature paint failure. The engineers that work on ventilation systems try to incorporate techniques to control moisture for building, renovating, and maintaining a structure. Good ventilation can protect the building's occupants from unpleasant odors, irritating pollutants, and potentially dangerous gases.

- Programmable thermostats—Using engineer-designed programmable thermostats is one of the easiest ways to save energy in a home. An ENERGY STAR qualified programmable thermostat helps make it easy for homeowners to save by regulating temperatures in all seasons.

- New and better forms of insulation keep homes warm in the winter and cool in the summer.

- High-efficiency light bulbs and lighting controls automatically turn lights on and off and reduce electricity demands.

- High-efficiency windows, doors, and skylights reduce the amount of energy needed to maintain a comfortable temperature and amount of light.

Green buildings are being constructed all over the globe. You can search for green buildings in your area in the US Department of Energy's High Performance Buildings Database. Two of the most commonly used green building rating systems are the Green Building Council's Leadership in Energy and Environmental Design (LEED) and the Green Building Initiative's (GBI) Green Globes. USGBC maintains a database of LEED-registered or certified building projects.

An Interview with Kellie Stokes, Energy Research Engineer at Appalachian Energy Center

1. How did you first learn about your field? Was it your intention to have a "green" career?
   Early on I recognized in myself a sort of split-brain

phenomenon where I loved both technical and creative pursuits, especially design. After getting my undergrad in math and art, I was drawn to architecture as a way to marry the two, and spent two years at the Auburn University Rural Studio designing and building a low-income housing prototype for the Alabama Black Belt Heritage Area. I loved this work and wondered how I could continue to work on the technical side of design, while still making a difference in the world after leaving the Rural Studio. During a lecture, I was introduced to the concept of an Environmental Designer, a communication bridge between architects and engineers that helps define the environmental targets and pushes the environmental performance of a building. It had all the right pieces—technically challenging, creative, and important.

2. Where did you go to school? What kind of degree do you have?
   Dartmouth College- BA in math and Studio Art
   MIT- MS in Mechanical Engineering

3. What do you do now? What is your day like?
   I am now working as a Research Engineer at the Appalachian Energy Center. I get to work on the research side of the environmental performance of buildings. I like research because it's constantly new—the problems you encounter are often problems no one else has encountered before. I want to transform the way our built environment uses natural resources, and a lot of that transformation first happens through research.

4. What advice do you have for students that are interested in becoming a green engineer? Do you recommend it? What skills are most important to be good at your job?
   I absolutely recommend it. Even during this economic recession, it's a field that's growing and constantly

changing. No longer are engineers just number crunchers, they have to be excellent communicators, team players, technically-savvy, and have big picture perspective. For my job, in particular, you have to be able to talk to people from varied backgrounds—contractors, designers, building owners, scientists-- and help them understand key issues outside of their fields. You also have to have some entrepreneurial skills.

5. What's your favorite part of the job?
   My favorite part of the job is feeling so relevant to the urgent important issues facing our country right now. When you read the newspapers, so much of what we struggle with as a country is related to energy—our international relationships, our economic health, our politics on climate change. Green engineers are optimists—they're problem solvers, not just problem identifiers. I feel like I'm part of the solution in a uniquely nerdy way.

6. What is the worst part?
   For green engineering, I think it's getting to where you want to be. Engineering is an extremely broad field, and it's easy to get lost among all the options and start working on something you're not that excited about because you know it will pay the bills. Unlike becoming a doctor or a lawyer, there's no real traditional track for green engineers, and there are few role models since it's a relatively new area. You kind of have to pave your own path, which at times that can be daunting.

7. If you could do it all over again, what, if anything, would you change and why?
   I think I might have gone straight into my PhD after getting my masters. I knew, even then, that I wanted to teach and do research, so I could have jumpstarted my career a little earlier. I've applied for PhD programs for

next year, hoping to expand my focus area beyond the building envelope to look at urban resource use, but it's just happening a little later than I had originally hoped.

If you are interested in creating healthy homes, work and recreational spaces, there are plenty of opportunities for a great career as a green building engineer. In the design of green building, the most common engineers are heating ventilating and air-conditioning (HVAC), architectural, civil, environmental, electrical, and mechanical engineers. Most of these engineers are LEED certified, and have the pleasure of knowing that their work is helping millions of people become healthier and leave less of an impact on the environment.

LEADERSHIP IN ENERGY AND ENVIRONMENTAL DESIGN (LEED)
LEED certification provides independent verification that a building, home, or community was designed and built using strategies aimed at achieving high performance in key areas of human and environmental health. These areas are sustainable site development, water savings, energy efficiency, materials selection, and indoor environmental quality. In other words, the LEED rating systems looks at how much energy and water is consumed within the building, the indoor air quality, and the use of renewable materials. LEED provides a framework for identifying and implementing practical and measurable green building design, construction, operations, and maintenance solutions.

LEED is perhaps the best known rating system in the U.S. but it is not the only one. Energy-Star and Green Globes are some of the others.

THE ENGINEERS WHO HELP DESIGN GREEN BUILDINGS

- Architectural Engineers consider the forces of hurricane winds, snow, or earthquakes. They concern themselves with mechanical systems of buildings; such as regulating interior air flow, determining wall thickness, choosing materials, and designing interior and exterior heat sources. They also plan plumbing, heating, and air conditioning, as well as electrical and lighting systems. Architectural engineers may manage construction projects by focusing on the safety, cost, and construction methods.

- Civil and Structural Engineers specify the actual structure of the building, including green roofing systems and thermal performance. They often work with the architectural engineer to make sure the building does not move under any circumstances.

- Heating Ventilating and Air-Conditioning (HVAC) Engineers design the heating, ventilating and air-conditioning systems within the building.

- Electrical Engineers may optimize energy performance by performing energy audits, researching alternatives, and implementing alternative energy solutions. They may also design the lighting, computer networks, and distribution of electricity within the building.

- Environmental Engineers develop cleanup or remediation programs and countermeasures in case of mishaps. They clean up asbestos and mold, and perform inspections, planning, and oversight during the design and construction of the green building. They may also prepare Indoor Air Quality (IAQ) management plans and environmental impact studies for regulatory agencies.

- Geological Engineers assist in creating a sediment and erosion (due to storm-water runoff) control plan, and help prevent pollution from dust and other particles.

- Materials Engineers assist in the certification of hardwoods, plywood, medium density fiberboard, and particle board.
- Mechanical Engineers are responsible for all mechanical systems within a building. They may also manage the construction process and make sure the job stays on time and on budget. They may also perform inspections and evaluations of equipment and systems for proper installation, troubleshooting, and improvement.

Chapter Four

Natural Resources Management

Fresh air to breathe, clean water to drink, and healthy food to eat involves the work of many types of engineers—environmental, civil, chemical, manufacturing, agricultural and, biological engineers. It is easy to take healthy air, water, and food for granted

if you have never been exposed to people or places without them, but they are critical to life on this planet.

Once upon a time, the solution to unhealthy air, water, and food would have been to consume, pollute, and discard less. But now, we want to create a sustainable way of life that not only stops the damage caused by industrialization, but also reverses it. If you want to be a part of the solution to eliminate toxins that pollute the air and water, which eventually end up in our food and then our bodies, there are abundant engineering jobs that offer challenges and the satisfaction of knowing that you are making a difference in the world. According to Gay Taylor, President of The Taylor Waller Company, "Every aspect of life on this earth from space travel to entertainment to transportation to harvesting and producing food has had an engineer impact it in some way." Because new solutions to problems are always on the horizon, you'll need to be a curious person and a life-long learner to succeed.

Conchita Jimenez-Gonzales, a graduate in environmental engineering from the Monterrey Institute of Technology (ITESM, Mexico) said, "As I was going through college I saw very quickly that it is more intelligent to prevent waste instead of cleaning it up, so I decided to apply those chemical engineering techniques to help design processes that are greener from the beginning. In my mind, green engineering is doing engineering the right way from the beginning—it is all about changing behaviors. Whether they are in the 'green' jobs area or in a traditional engineering job, engineers can always make things safer, greener, and more efficient."

"All sectors of the global community are involved in some form of waste management. The human densities of today's urban zones presents increased challenges of dealing with vast volumes of waste, be it municipal, sewage, water drainage, organic compost, or recyclable materials. Rural areas produce less waste but often suffer from a poorly developed waste management system. The challenge for today's waste management teams is both to reduce the amount of waste entering the system and to develop the protocols and processes required to achieve 100-percent recycling of all future waste."

– from www.greenenergyjobs.com

Waste Management

Waste management is important to preserving our environment. Cleaning up, restoring, and protecting the environment is estimated to be a $400 billion per year industry around the world. That's a lot of job opportunities for industrious and conscientious engineers. As our population continues to grow, this sector will become even more critical to continuing life as we know it.

Over the last three decades, public awareness of environmental problems has increased. Now, stricter federal regulations regarding the siting, construction, daily operation, and closure and post-closure monitoring of landfills have been developed. But, the amount of municipal solid waste generated in the United States has increased at a faster rate than our population growth. Climate change, over harvesting, species extinction, habitat disruption, pollution, and other detrimental influences are all very real concerns that need dedicated and passionate engineers to find and manage the solutions.

The Environmental Protection Agency (EPA) has collected and reported data on the generation and disposal of waste in the US for more than 30 years to measure the success of waste reduction and recycling programs across the country. In 2010, Americans generated about 250 million tons of trash, and recycled and composted over 85 million tons of material, which is equivalent to a 34.1 percent recycling rate. On average, each American recycled and composted 1.51 pounds out of the 4.43 pounds of waste generation per day.

Do you know where your trash and recyclables are taken? Have you ever visited a landfill? What did people do before there were plastic bags, aluminum cans, or trash removal services?

The amount of natural resources we throw away is another part of the solid-waste problem that is not always apparent. Even though we're recycling tons of metals, glass, plastic, and paper, we need to move beyond recycling and do more to reduce waste before it is produced.

THE ENGINEERS WHO WORK IN WASTE MANAGEMENT

- Chemical and Materials Engineers may research materials and processes used ways to develop products that can be reused, recycled or reinvented, and thereby eliminate waste.
- Civil Engineers are the backbone of waste management. They are involved in assessing each community's specific needs by determining its population size and density, future growth projections, and environmental concerns. They inspect the current system capacity, integrity, and location, as well the budget needed to expand or build new.
- Environmental Engineers protect people and the environment by limiting toxic materials. They assess the processes used during product development and study

the potential impact on the environment. They may also prepare environmental impact studies for regulatory agencies.

PRODUCT LIFECYCLES

Making products environmentally friendly is a top priority for green engineers. Every product available in stores has made some impact on the environment. Many products are made from natural resources and are transported to stores across the United States. The product may include packaging, and may be used anywhere from one time to several years.

Just as living things are born, age, and die, products also have a life cycle. Each stage of a product's development affects our environment in different ways—from how we use it to the quantities of it we buy. What we do with a product when we are finished with it also has environmental effects.

According to the EPA, a product's life cycle usually includes the following stages:

1. Design—Engineers, designers, manufacturers, and others get ideas for products and then manufacture them. Most product designs are researched and tested before being mass-produced. A product's initial design affects each stage of its life cycle and therefore, its impact on our environment. For example, products designed to be reused instead of thrown out prevent waste and conserve natural resources.

2. Materials acquisition—Whether synthetic or naturally occurring, all products are made from raw materials. Virgin materials (those being used or worked for the first time) such as trees or iron ore, are directly harvested or mined from the earth. Using these materials requires large amounts of energy and depletes our natural resources. Making new products from materials that were used in another product (called recycled or recovered materials)

can reduce pollution, energy use, and the amount of raw materials needed from the earth.

3. Materials processing—When materials are extracted from the earth, they must be converted into a form that can be used to make products. For example, trees contribute the wood from which paper is made. The wood is made into paper after several different manufacturing processes. Each process creates waste and consumes energy. Making one ton of recycled paper uses 64 percent less energy, uses 50 percent less water; creates 74 percent less air pollution; saves 17 trees; and creates five times more jobs than does manufacturing one ton of paper from virgin wood pulp.

4. Manufacturing—Products are made in factories that use a great deal of energy. Manufacturing processes also create waste and often contribute to the production of greenhouse gases. Glass beverage containers, for example, can be used over and over an infinite number of times. More than 41 billion glass containers are made each year. Recycling just one of those containers saves enough energy to light a 100-watt bulb for four hours. Imagine the energy savings from recycling all 41 billion containers. What's more, making one ton of glass from 50 percent recycled materials saves 250 pounds of mining waste.

5. Packaging—Many products are packaged in paper or plastic, which also undergo separate manufacturing processes that use energy and consume natural resources. While packaging can serve several important functions, such as preventing tampering, providing information, and preserving hygienic integrity and freshness, sometimes packaging is excessive.

A particular problem with plastic is that it is not biodegradeable. Plastics often end up in water systems and harm wildlife. Birds have eaten foam pellets after mistaking them for fish eggs floating on the water and waterfowl have become entangled in the plastic loops often used to hold beverage bottles and cans together. Both can have deadly consequences.

6. Distribution—Manufactured products are transported in trucks, planes, trains, and ships to different locations where they are sold. Materials and parts used to make products are also transported to different places at earlier stages in the life cycle. All of this transporting uses energy and generates greenhouse gases.

7. Use—The way products are used impacts our environment. Reusable, durable, and recyclable products conserve natural resources, use less energy, and create less waste than disposable, single-use products. For example, fluorescent light bulbs reduce energy consumption because they are four to five times more efficient than incandescent light bulbs. Reducing energy use cuts down on power plant emissions that contribute to greenhouse gases, acid precipitation, and smog. Properly caring for products also increases their useful life, so remember to read and follow the cleaning, operating, and maintenance instructions for the products you own, especially tires on bicycles and other vehicles. By extending the life of your products, you make a direct impact on decreasing demands on natural resources.

8. Reuse/Recycle—Recycling or remanufacturing products into new ones saves energy and reduces the amount of raw materials that have to be used in the manufacturing process. When products are reused or recycled, their life does not end. Instead, it becomes a continuous cycle. For example, one pound of recycled paper can make six new cereal boxes, and five recycled plastic bottles can make enough fiberfill to stuff a ski jacket.

9. Disposal—Throwing products in the trash ends their useful life. We simply lose these valuable resources. If the United States recycled all its morning newspapers, we could save 41,000 trees a day and keep six million tons

of waste out of landfills. The same benefits are true if all newspapers switched to online delivery.

THE LIFE CYCLE OF A **CD** OR **DVD**

You listen to them on your stereo, play them in your computer, or watch movies on them. Compact discs (CDs) and their cousins, digital video discs (DVDs) and BlueRays, are everywhere! Only a few millimeters thick, they provide hours of entertainment and hold huge volumes of information.

Do you ever stop to think about how disks are made, what materials are used, or what happens to these discs when you don't want them any more?

Making products like CDs and DVDs consumes natural resources, produces waste, and uses energy. By learning about product life cycles, you can find out how to reduce the environmental impact and natural resources used to make products you use every day. When you understand these connections, you can make better environmental choices about the products you use and how you dispose of them. The life cycle of a CD or DVD includes the following:

1. Materials acquisition—CDs and DVDs are made from many different materials, each of which has its own life cycle involving energy use and waste. The materials include:

   - Aluminum—The most abundant metal element in the earth's crust; bauxite ore is the main source of aluminum and is extracted from the earth.
   - Polycarbonate—A type of plastic made from crude oil and natural gas extracted from the earth.
   - Lacquer—Made of acrylic, which is another type of plastic.
   - Gold—A metal mined from the earth.
   - Dyes—Chemicals made in a laboratory, partially from petroleum products that come from the earth

- Other materials such as water, glass, silver, and nickel.

2. Materials processing—Most mined materials must be processed before manufacturers can use them to make CDs or DVDs. For example:

   - Bauxite ore is processed into a substance called alumina by washing, crushing, dissolving, filtering, and harvesting the materials. Alumina is then turned into aluminum through a process called smelting. Then, the metal is shaped, rolled, or made into a cast.
   - To make plastics, crude oil from the ground is combined with natural gas and chemicals in a manufacturing or processing plant.

3. Manufacturing—The manufacturing process is essentially the same for CDs and DVDs.

   - An injection-molding machine creates the core of the disc that is a one-millimeter-thick piece of polycarbonate (plastic). Polycarbonate is melted and put in a mold. With several tons of pressure, a stamper embeds tiny indentations, or pits, with digital information into the plastic mold. A CD player's laser reads these pits when playing a CD.
   - Next, the plastic mold goes through the metallizer machine, which coats the CDs with a thin, reflective layer of metal (usually aluminum) through a process called sputtering. The playback laser reads the information off the reflective aluminum surface.
   - The CD receives a layer of lacquer as protective coating against scratching and corrosion.
   - Most CDs are screen printed with one to five different colors for a decorative label. Screen printing uses many materials including stencils, squeegees, and inks.

4. Packaging—CDs and DVDs are packaged in clear or colored plastic cases (jewel cases) or cardboard boxes that are covered with plastic shrink-wrap. This packaging can be made from recycled or raw materials. For example, the plastic used can be from recycled bottles, or from crude oil and natural gas extracted from the earth and combined with chemicals.

5. Distribution—When discs are packaged, they are ready to be sent to distribution centers, retail outlets, or other locations. Transportation by plane, truck, or rail requires the use of fossil fuels for energy. These fossil fuels are not renewable.

6. Use—CDs and DVDs are created with materials that are extremely stable. If properly stored and handled, most discs will last for decades and probably centuries. Certain conditions, such as high humidity, extended periods of high temperatures, rapid temperature changes, and exposure to certain types of light, can damage discs and shorten their useful life. Taking care of your discs by keeping them out of direct sunlight and away from heat and water will help them last longer. Not only will you save money, but you will also reduce the discs' environmental impacts by preventing waste.

7. Reuse/Recycle—Depending on their condition, discs can be reused or recycled instead of thrown away. CDs can be recycled for use in new products. Specialized electronic recycling companies clean, grind, blend, and compound the discs into a high-quality plastic for a variety of uses, including the following:
   - Automotive industry parts.
   - Raw materials to make plastics (discs are ground into a gravel-like substance, which is sold to companies that melt it down and convert it to plastic).
   - Office equipment.

- Alarm boxes and panels, streetlights, and electrical cable insulation.
- Jewel cases that hold CDs.

Most CD recycling companies only accept large stockpiles of old, damaged, or unused CDs and DVDs from businesses. A few companies will accept smaller quantities of discs mailed by individuals. When recyclers receive the CDs, they separate the packaging materials, manuals, and CDs for individual recycling processes. For more information, visit the CD Recycling Center of America at www.cdrecyclingcenter.com

As with most stages of product life cycles, even recycling has environmental trade-offs. CD and DVD recycling is now an emerging technology, which means that many companies are not yet capable of recycling these discs. So, while recycling CDs and DVDs saves natural resources, the trade-off comes from the amount of fuel and energy that is consumed to transport discs long distances to an appropriate recycling facility.

8. Disposal—Only dispose of discs when you have no other choice. Always try to share, donate, or trade discs, or drop them off at an appropriate recycling center. CDs and DVDs that are thrown away waste energy and result in lost valuable resources.

As you see, even a simple everyday item has a large environmental impact. With this realization, you might ask the question, "is the true cost of manufacturing, packaging, distribution and life cycle covered in a 50 cent disk?" Green engineers are concerned with including the true cost for the life of the product. Including health risks to the people and ecosystems at the production sites, gold mines and other extraction and disposal sites. Many studies have found that if the total cost of goods and products like production, transportation, remediation, health care and disposal were included in the purchase price, then consumer demand would be greatly curbed. In addition, longer lasting and safer products would be manufactured.

Fresh Air

Air pollution is a problem worldwide. According to the World Health Organization, 70,000 people in the United States die from air pollution every year. That is twice as many as those who die in traffic accidents.

Air quality has different effects on plants, animals, and humans. In humans, poor air quality can lead to cancer, asthma, poor quality of life, and birth defects. Under the Clean Air Act, the EPA established air quality standards to protect public health, including the health of "sensitive" populations such as people with asthma, children, and older adults. The EPA also sets secondary standards to protect public welfare. These include protecting ecosystems from harm, as well as protecting against decreased visibility and damage to crops, vegetation, and buildings.

Cleaning the air is usually a job for environmental engineers. Environmental engineers use the principles of biology and chemistry to develop solutions to environmental problems. They are involved in water and air pollution control, recycling, waste disposal, and public health issues. Environmental engineers conduct hazardous-waste management studies in which they evaluate the significance of the hazard, advise on its treatment and containment, and develop regulations to prevent mishaps. They design municipal water supply and industrial wastewater treatment systems, conduct research on the environmental impact of proposed construction projects, analyze scientific data, and perform quality-control checks.

Environmental engineers are concerned with local and worldwide environmental issues. Some may study and attempt to minimize the effects of acid precipitation, global climate change, automobile emissions, and ozone depletion. They also may be involved in the protection of wildlife and ecology studies.

Many environmental engineers work as consultants, helping their clients to comply with regulations, prevent environmental damage, and clean up hazardous sites.

When pollution comes from human activities and industrial production in particular, it may require the development of major abatement or cleaning technologies. However, environmental engineers must always balance the cost of cleanup with the degree of abatement achieved. These engineers must be excellent communicators and team players. They must able to work well with others because their work often includes collaborating with environmental scientists, urban planners, hazardous waste technicians, politicians, attorneys, and other specialists. They prepare, review, and update environmental investigations, provide clean-up recommendations, monitor projects, prepare forecasts and budgets, and inspect sites to ensure operational effectiveness and compliance.

Engineers concerned with air pollution usually research, design, plan, or perform engineering duties in the prevention, control, and remediation of environmental hazards. They may also develop or propose projects, collect data, obtain plans and permits, and advise industries, corporations, and government agencies. They advise on environmental policies and procedures as well as the best way to clean up contaminated sites to protect people and the environment.

For example, environmental engineers that design buildings in zoos often need to determine if diseases are communicable to either animals or people. What diseases are airborne and what animals are susceptible to them? Some species of animals can get sick from people, and people can get sick from some animals. Because bats carry rabies, people are prevented from breathing the same air as the bats by separate air-handling systems. These systems include pressurization, humidity control, heating, ventilation, and cooling. The size of each area must be analyzed, and systems are developed to keep the people and animals safe.

THE ENGINEERS WHO HELP DESIGN FRESH AIR

- Environmental and Civil Engineers protect people and the environment by limiting toxic materials, conducting hazardous-waste management studies, and developing regulations to prevent mishaps. Some study and attempt to minimize the effects of acid precipitation, global climate change, automobile emissions, and ozone depletion.
- Heating Ventilating and Air-Conditioning (HVAC) Engineers design, evaluate, and maintain indoor air quality.
- Mechanical Engineers may develop air filtration and purification systems or products.

Fresh Water

Clean water has been an issue for thousands of years, and ancient Egyptian and Sanskrit writings mention desalinization as far back as 2000 BC. The first ideas for designing clean water systems took hold in the 1600's amidst one of the worst periods of plague in history. The resulting improvement on the quality of life through clean water development all over the world was remarkable.

According to the United Nations, every person on earth requires 20–50 liters of clean, safe water a day for drinking, cooking, and keeping themselves clean. Polluted water is deadly. 1.8 million people die from water-related illnesses every year, and tens of millions are seriously sickened by preventable water-related ailments. In fact, lack of clean water is responsible for more deaths in the world than war. About 1 out of every 6 people living today does not have adequate access to water. The World Health Organization estimates that nearly 5,000 children die worldwide from water born diarrhea-related diseases each day.

Engineers are desperately needed to tackle this problem. The United Nations warns that, "Overcoming the crisis in water and sanitation is one of the greatest human development challenges of the early 21st century." The National Academy of Engineering has also listed access to safe drinking water as one of the grand challenges for engineers of the 21st century. The key term here is "access," which is the real challenge. For example, Canada has more drinking water than its people can consume, but other countries such as Northern Africa and Saudi Arabia are in a constant state of drought. Water in the oceans makes up 73 percent of the planet, but because of the salt, it is not drinkable. And in some developing countries, water supplies are contaminated not only by the people discharging toxic contaminants, but also by arsenic and other naturally occurring pollutants from groundwater aquifers. Chemicals from human and animal wastes, agricultural runoff, and industrial chemicals can also make water unsafe to drink. If engineers can solve the problem of providing worldwide access to clean water, it would save million of lives and become one of the greatest achievements of human kind.

There are four important characteristics of drinking water supplies:
- Quality,
- Quantity,
- Reliability, and
- Cost.

To solve these problems, engineers are hard at work designing more efficient:
- Desalination systems to create drinking water from ocean water by removing the salt. Currently, there are about 12,000 desalination plants worldwide, but they are very expensive to build and have prohibitive energy needs.
- Ways to transport water from locations where it is abundant to locations where it is scarce.
- Recycling waste and gray water so that it can be used for non-personal uses such as irrigation or industrial purposes.

- Helping businesses and consumers reduce use by designing low-flow toilet and faucets and high-efficiency shower heads for homes, and drip-irrigation systems for crops and agricultural purposes.
- Distillation systems to remove contaminants from any water source. A unit smaller than a dishwasher could provide daily clean water for 100 people.

Civil and environmental engineers are making sure we have good quality water resources that ensure safe drinking water. They work in water regulation, monitoring and water treatment plant design, waste management and cleanup, and pollution prevention.

Often, assessing the water quality of a stream, river, or swamp is a matter of common sense. If the quality of the water is good, you will see an abundance of fish, plants, and insects. If the quality of the water is poor, it is likely to smell bad, appear cloudy and you may even see trash and pollution on the surface. Don't swim in this water! However, bacteria and microbiological organisms that you can't see can also cause disease. There are many stories about hikers and campers getting sick from clean-looking river water, so never assume that it is clean.

In the civil and environmental engineering world, healthy drinking water is made by cleaning it. Water treatment plants typically clean water by aerating, removing sediment, filtering, and then disinfecting it. But other cleaning options are also available. A South Bronx community group plans to reseed their waterway with oysters and mussels in an effort to clean up their polluted waters. The oysters won't be fit for human consumption, but could help clean a waterway which has been devastated by dumping, sewage and landfill. Because the bivalves (mussels and oysters) are filter feeders—sucking in water and slurping algae and plankton from it—a square foot of oysters can filter 2,000 gallons of water per day.

Everyone on the planet can help improve the quality of our water by being mindful of the activities that we do at home.

By not purchasing hazardous household cleaning products, and never dumping chemicals such as pesticides, fuels, and fertilizers in yards and storm-drains, we can reduce the pollution that poisons our watersheds and prevents water treatment plants from easily cleaning our water. Essentially, if we don't pollute, we are helping the system.

Abena Scakey Ojetayo, a graduate of the Civil Infrastructure and Sustainable Development program at Cornell University, and Infrastructure Planner and Project Engineer for the Anam New City Project (a model sustainable city project in West Africa) said, "The time has come when sustainable engineering is no longer an option. Prospective 'green engineers' need to care and be interested in ideas and issues outside of formulas and theorems. Being 'green' requires interdisciplinary thinking and problem solving. They make it a habit to poke their nose in other fields (especially urban planning and international development—the world is now a global village)."

According to the EPA, the most common sources of storm water pollutants are:

- Silt, sand, and clay—Commons sources are construction sites, bare spots in lawns and gardens, wastewater with particles and other debris from washing cars and trucks in driveways or parking lots, dirt roads and driveways, and unprotected stream banks and drainage ways.
- Nutrients—Common sources are fertilizers, pet waste, grass clippings and leaves left on streets and sidewalks, leaves burned in ditches, and atmospheric deposition.
- Disease organisms—Common sources are pet and wildlife waste and garbage.
- Hydrocarbons—Common sources are car and truck exhaust, leaks and spills of oil and gas, dumping of used oil, and burning leaves and garbage.
- Pesticides—Common sources are pesticides over-applied or applied before a rainstorm, and spills and leaks.

- Metals—Common sources are cars and trucks from brake and tire wear and exhaust, galvanized metal gutters and downspouts, and industrial activities.

Storm sewers are designed to carry storm water directly to streams or other bodies of water. For many years, people thought that storm water was delivered to water treatment plants. Unfortunately, everything in the path of the rainwater runoff will go directly into your local water system. The contaminants can kill fish and wildlife, ruin the natural nutrient balance of the water, contaminate drinking water, and make swimming or any other form of recreation unsafe.

In addition to fresh water sources being endangered by contamination, oceans as a food source are also endangered. It is estimated that 50% of the world's oceans have been contaminated by oil spills.

THE ENGINEERS WHO HELP DESIGN CLEAN WATER

- Environmental and Civil Engineers are at the forefront protecting people and the environment by limiting toxic materials, conducting water management studies, and developing regulations to prevent mishaps. Some work in water regulation, monitoring and water treatment plant design, waste management and cleanup, and pollution prevention.

Healthy Food

Take a walk down any aisle in your local grocery store. What most people don't realize is that behind every product on every shelf are engineers that work to make that food taste good and healthy. Every aspect of food production, processing, marketing, and distribution benefits from engineering. In fact, 20 percent of Americans work in agriculture, and it is one of the most diverse industries. Creating machines to do agricultural work is considered one of the greatest engineering achievements of the 20th century.

Food engineers are involved in all aspects of food preparation and processing. They influence the packaging, storage, and distribution systems of foods as varied as candy bars and frozen dinners. Because new products and environmentally friendly food-processing equipment need to be developed, engineers are in high demand within the food industry.

Food engineering pertains to the properties and characteristics of foods that affect their processing. Food engineering requires an understanding of the chemical, biochemical, microbiological, and physical characteristics of food. There will be a shortage of food engineers as long as society demands that engineers develop lower-fat, lower-salt, lower-cholesterol, or nutrient-packed foods for their diets.

Agricultural and biological engineers are also working to ensure foods are healthy and will have no adverse effects on humans after consumption. Agricultural and biological engineering, two closely integrated disciplines which together are often called biological systems (biosystems), bioresources, or natural resources engineering, are concerned with finding solutions for life on our small planet. As an agricultural engineer, you could create new technology for agricultural systems, materials, and products that will help provide high-quality and affordable food and fiber for the world's billions of people. Every aspect of food production, processing, marketing, and distribution can benefit from your expertise.

Bioresource engineers devise practical, efficient solutions for producing, storing, transporting, processing, and packaging agricultural products. They solve problems related to systems, processes and machines that interact with humans, plants, animals, microorganisms and biological materials. They develop solutions for responsible, innovative uses of agricultural products and natural resources, including soil, water, air and energy. And they do all this with a constant eye toward improved protection of people, animals, and the environment.

Agricultural engineers are also involved in research and development (R&D). They investigate ways and methods that can help plants survive in hostile environments. They work in alternative energy research looking for ways to make fuels from renewable resources like grain. They produce computer models of plant and animal systems, and they also do research into advanced machinery and equipment that will increase efficiency and effectively manage different aspects of the agricultural industry.

According to The American Society of Agricultural and Biological Engineers (ASABE), there are eleven technical divisions that define the industry:

1. Aquacultural Engineering
2. Biological Engineering
3. Education
4. Food and Process Engineering
5. Forest Engineering
6. Information and Electrical Technologies
7. Power and Machinery Engineering
8. Soil and Water Engineering
9. Structures and Environment Engineering
10. Ergonomic, Safety and Health
11. Energy

If you think of engineers as problem solvers, you can think of agricultural engineer solving problems such as these:

	Problem	**Solution**
1.	Increased population means less land is available for farming.	Agricultural engineers are hard at work developing alternative growing conditions for plants such as hydrophonics and soil-less agriculture.

| 2 | Storage facilities are needed for farmers. | Agricultural engineers design and manufacture farm structures such as healthy barns for livestock and facilities for storing grain, hay, and feed. They also strive to improve the housing and living conditions for farm workers and their families. |
| 3 | People around the world are suffering from hunger. | Agricultural engineers work with other countries to improve farming practices in countries with very little land and many people to feed. |

THE ENGINEERS WHO HELP DESIGN HEALTHY FOOD

- Agricultural and Biological Engineers may create new technology for agricultural systems, materials, and products that will help provide high-quality and affordable food and fiber. They may also be involved in every aspect of food production, processing, marketing, and distribution.
- Chemical and Food Engineers are involved in every aspect of food production, processing, marketing, and distribution. Food engineers are involved in everything that pertains to the properties and characteristics of foods that affect their processing.
- Environmental Engineers participate in the food industry to protect people and the environment by limiting toxic materials. They assess the processes used during harvesting and study the potential impact on the storage and transportation of food.
- Mechanical Engineers design, manufacture, and inspect farming equipment that makes a farmer or farm system more efficient. They may also research ways to improve production or harvesting techniques while lowering the cost.

Chapter Five

Biomimicry - Biological Systems Design From Nature

Biomimicry uses the genius of nature to design materials and products. For example, Velcro came about when a Swiss agricultural engineer noticed burs on his pants and dog's fur after a hike. Since then Velcro has been used in household, industrial, space, and medical applications. Engineers also created sharkskin swimsuits for Olympic swimmers after studying the Mako shark's skin to determine why they are the fastest fish in the world.

Biomimicry is an exciting multidisciplinary field for any person interested in biology, sustainability, and engineering. The applications are virtually limitless, and you can be almost any type of engineer. If you find that you are inspired by the natural world, enjoy interacting or observing plants and animals, and want to make a difference in the world, this may be the field for you.

Biomimicry, or biologically inspired engineering is exactly that—engineering that gets its inspiration from adaptations in the natural world. These engineers study living organisms and systems to understand how they have adapted. According to Tom Muller, author of *Biomimetics: Design by Nature*, nature is very complex and "the multilayered character of much natural engineering makes it particularly difficult to penetrate

111

and pluck apart. The gecko's feet work so well not just because of their billions of tiny nanohairs, but also because those hairs grow on larger hairs, which in turn grow on toe ridges that are part of bigger toe pads, and so on. Engineers are hard at work to reproduce these intricate nanopuzzles while Nature assembles them effortlessly, molecule by molecule."

There are about 1400 applications of biomimicry in the world today (according to asknature.org). Everything from the adhesive proteins of mussels (glue) to pest control products based on chemicals that termites use for defense, to the stems of bamboo that are teaching civil engineers how to resist buckling under structural loads, the applications in this field are only limited by your imagination. Some of the first lunar robots were modeled after insects and one even resembles a crab. Nature is all around us and is an inspiring teacher in this field.

EXAMPLES OF BIOMIMICRY IN ACTION

Below are seven examples of amazing biomimicry applications. This list doesn't even scratch the surface of everything that engineers can do in this field, but serve as a launching pad for your imagination.

1. Termite Ingenuity—Termites build spectacular structures. Throughout the savanna ecosystems, they build their mounds to maintain a constant temperature. Much like a passive solar design, their structures stay cool in the day and release heat during the night to maintain a constant temperature. Termites do this by opening and closing channels and shafts (vents) throughout the mound to manage convection currents of air. These principles inspired the design of the Eastgate Center in Harare, Zimbabwe, which uses only 35 percent of the energy of similar buildings.

2. Gecko Bandages—If you have even wanted to climb walls or hang upside down from the ceiling by your fingertips

you may now be in luck with gecko bandages. According to Asknature.org, "Scientists at the Massachusetts Institute of Technology have created a surgical bandage that mimics the way that gecko feet can adhere to vertical surfaces. The bandage could be used for both applications both outside and inside the body, such as to repair tears, prevent leaks, and replace sutures. The bandage would be a glue-coated polymer with the glue consisting of hundreds of thousands of nanopillars that provide high surface contact."

3. Whalepower Wind Turbine—WhalePower developed a new fan and wind turbine blade design using Tubercle Technology. This was inspired by the flippers of humpback whales, which have tubercles or bumps on the leading edges. Blades designed using Tubercle Technology are more energy efficient. The wind turbine blades require lower wind speeds, increasing the amount of time and the number of locations where they can actively generate electricity.

4. Lotus Effect Hydrophobia—Lotus plants are self-cleaning and stay free of dirt without using detergent or expending energy. The plant's cuticle uses wax to repel water and dirt. This amazing repelling surface structure has inspired the manufacturers of paints, glass, textiles, and more that reduce the need for chemical detergents and costly labor.

5. Car Collision Avoidance—Locusts, which can consume their own weight in food each day, have a large neuron called the locust giant movement detector (LGMD) located behind their eyes. The LGMD releases bursts of energy whenever a locust is on a collision course with another locust or a predatory bird. These spikes of energy, called action potentials, prompt the locusts to take evasive action. The entire process from motion detection to reaction takes about 45 milliseconds—or 45 thousandths of a second. And because the insects only detect things that are on a collision course with them, the locusts are

ignorant of all other movements. (Roach 2004) This technology is being developed by auto manufacturers for car-crash avoidance.

6. Bionic Car—DaimlerChrysler has developed a new concept car from Mercedes-Benz based on the shape of the tropical boxfish. Designers achieved an aerodynamic ideal that consumes 20 percent less fuel consumption, and has an 80 percent output reduction in nitrogen oxide emissions. The diesel-powered compact will get about 70 miles per gallon, and can run on biodiesel fuel, too.

7. RoboClam Anchor—The typical ship's anchor has been improved and completely changed by using the razor clam as a model. From Discovery News: "The RoboClam, as the device is called, digs itself into the ground in two ways, similar to how a razor clam digs. First, the RoboClam vibrates, changing the relatively solid seabed into a quicksand-like fluid that is easier to dig through. Then the two "shells" of the machine expand, locking the anchor in place, while a worm-like foot pushes down. Once the foot is embedded, the shells contract and the foot pulls the rest of the machine down. The researchers hope the RoboClam will eventually dig twice as far as a razor clam, which can reach depths of more than 28 inches at a rate of about 0.4 inches per second."

All engineers can design biomimicry applications, products and systems.

Chapter Six

Socially Responsible Engineering

It's not a surprise that green engineers are expected to be ethical and also socially responsible. In fact, all engineers are held to the highest standards of morality and honesty. Engineers design our infrastructure, power plants, communication systems, food and agricultural systems, national security systems, medical equipment, and many other critical systems. Because society trusts engineers to protect their health and safety, there is no room for dishonesty or unethical behavior in the profession.

Socially responsible engineering is engineering that is sensitive to environmental and ethical issues such as environmental damage and improper treatment of workers. Socially responsible engineers consider the impact on the quality of life of those who live near the facilities, plants, structures, and thoroughfares they design, and in the cities and communities they plan and build. Where projects are built, whom they serve, and how they will affect those who live near them are at the heart of every decision made by the socially responsible engineer.

The National Society for Professional Engineers has a Code of Ethics for Engineers that summarizes the responsibilities of the engineering profession as: *Engineering is an important and learned profession. As members of this profession, engineers are expected to exhibit the highest standards of honesty and integrity. Engineering has a direct and vital impact on the quality of life for all people. Accordingly, the services provided by engineers require honesty, impartiality, fairness, and equity, and must be dedicated to the protection of the public health, safety, and welfare. Engineers must perform under a standard*

115

of professional behavior that requires adherence to the highest principles of ethical conduct.

FUNDAMENTAL CANONS

Engineers, in the fulfillment of their professional duties, shall:

1. Hold paramount the safety, health, and welfare of the public.
2. Perform services only in areas of their competence.
3. Issue public statements only in an objective and truthful manner.
4. Act for each employer or client as faithful agents or trustees.
5. Avoid deceptive acts.
6. Conduct themselves honorably, responsibly, ethically, and lawfully so as to enhance the honor, reputation, and usefulness of the profession.

Becoming a professional engineer is an important step toward letting the public know that you are socially responsible, ethical, and honest. A professional engineer (PE) is one who has been licensed by the state. Just as attorneys need to pass the bar exam and doctors need to pass the state medical board exam, engineers need to pass an eight-hour written exam called the Principles and Practices of Engineering exam.

Generally to become a PE, you must graduate from an accredited university, work for four years under the guidance of a professional engineer, and pass the PE exam. Most states, however, offer a pre-registration certificate called the Engineer Intern to those who do not yet have four years of experience. You can obtain the Engineer Intern certificate by passing an eight-hour Fundamentals of Engineering (FE) test. The first half of the test challenges your general engineering skills. The last half pertains to a specific concentration in engineering such as chemical, civil, electrical, environmental, industrial, or mechanical. Although the certificate does not authorize the practice of engineering, it is the first step in the process for full registration. Then, after you gain four years of experience, you can take the PE examination. This test relates specifically to a major branch of engineering.

Although registration is not mandatory, there is a strong trend in the engineering community toward licensure. To be in private practice as a consulting engineer, licensure is a legal requirement. Many high-level government positions can be filled only by professional engineers, and many states now require university instructors to be registered PEs. Most employers expect that students fresh out of college will be well versed in the basics or fundamentals of engineering. Engineer Intern certification provides proof. The National Society of Professional Engineers has plenty of information pertaining to the rules and requirements of registration on their Web site: www.nspe.org.

ENGINEERS CREED

The engineers creed is a philosophy of service, and a statement of belief that is usually delivered at graduation and licensure ceremonies.

As a Professional Engineer, I dedicate my professional knowledge and skill to the advancement and betterment of human welfare.

I pledge:
- *To give the utmost of performance;*
- *To participate in none but honest enterprise;*
- *To live and work according to the laws of man and the highest standards of professional conduct;*
- *To place service before profit, the honor and standing of the profession before personal advantage, and the public welfare above all other*

considerations.

*In humility and with need for Divine Guidance,
I make this pledge.*

This creed was adopted by National Society of Professional Engineers in June 1954, and engineers have lived and worked by its noble words ever since.

A green engineer combines all of the above and includes ecological and natural resource protection.

Chapter Seven

Getting Started

When you work with other people, good communication is very important. Communication skills include the ability to listen, write clearly, and speak well. In addition to being good communicators, engineers need to be passionate, energetic, creative, and excited about their work. The green industry is always evolving and changing. Being a good engineer is so much

 more than being really smart. Take extra classes in technical writing, develop excellent presentation skills, choose an industry that makes you excited about your career, and commit yourself to being the best you can be. Four years in engineering school may not be enough. To succeed, focus your energy, meet your goals, pay attention to details, and push yourself to be creative.

Remember that this book is only one source of information to help you decide whether you want to become a green engineer. Right now, you should begin reading everything you can find about engineering, and talk to every engineer or engineering student you know about the challenges ahead and how to prepare for them. Attend a summer camp or program pertaining to engineering at your school. Obtaining this information now may save you lots of heartache if you decide later that you are on the wrong path.

If you want to work in the green industry, the most valuable thing you can do is to get practical hands-on experience. Get out and do the actual work. Take classes in solar technology or electronics in college, and learn the basics from a technical standpoint. Try to get down to the nuts and bolts of what you are learning, and then get out and do it. If you go to work for a manufacturer that experience will be invaluable because you'll be able to relate to the customer for the products you design, and will be able to talk on their level. And your experience will also be invaluable to the company, because you can bring hands-on, practical information back to the company from actually knowing how to use the products that the company makes.

David Helgerson, the technical director for CSC's Advanced Marine Center says,

"I would advise students to gain as much practical experience as possible before and during school; this helps them understand the opportunities that will present themselves, will make more opportunities available, will provide money and will differentiate the student from other students with less experience. In high school, I would look for internships. In college I would look for intern opportunities in other geographic areas because moving when young is easier than later. I am a Professional Engineer and recommend becoming licensed. I also strongly recommend active participation in professional societies".

Academic preparation is also essential to exploring engineering as a career. In addition to coursework, getting involved in extracurricular activities pertaining to engineering can give you invaluable exposure. In high school, classes in algebra I and II, trigonometry, biology, physics, calculus, chemistry, computer programming, or computer applications can tell you if you have the aptitude and determination to study engineering. These courses are not all required to get into every engineering school, but early preparation can mean the difference between spending four years in college or six. Some universities also require two to three classes in a foreign language for admission.

Check into the programs that interest you and begin to fulfill their requirements. Advance Placement (AP) or Honors courses are recommended, as well as an ACT score of 20 or a SAT score of at least 1000.

BECOME WELL-ROUNDED

Companies want to hire engineers who are well-rounded, work well in teams, and communicate effectively. When it comes to inspiration, conceptualization, and rock-solid prototypes that really work, every engineering discipline is important. Every engineering student today must study multiple disciplines so they can be well-rounded and very creative in their thinking. You may find yourself working with other engineers, scientists, private entrepreneurs, inventors, investors, technicians, urban planners, accountants, politicians, and policy makers. The collective knowledge of the entire group may be needed to deal with a serious problem.

It's like playing in a band—the guitarist sets the bass line or melody, the drummer sets the rhythm, and the singer adds words and meaning. Beautiful music is made by each person doing what they do best, and by working together. Each player brings different strengths to the band, and the band can't make great music without each part. Teamwork is integral to the success of the band. Engineering design works in the same way. Each member of the team contributes according to his or her individual strengths, and as a result, society gets new or more sustainable products, benefits from improved renewable energy sources, and an increased quality of life.

COMMUNICATION SKILLS

Are communication skills necessary? Absolutely! Rarely do people work alone. Any engineer must be able to tell other people what is happening, what to expect, and what is needed, verbally or in writing. Specifications, proposals, briefings, and reports are all part of the job.

Learn to communicate effectively—you won't regret it.

SUMMER CAMPS

Summer camps provide another innovative approach to preparing for a career in engineering or evaluating if that career is right for you. Find out what it is like to study engineering; learn about the different types of engineers and what engineers do on a daily basis. Almost every college of engineering offers a summer engineering camp for high-school students. These camps offer a week or two of fun while developing leadership, professional, and personal organizational skills, and they provide opportunities to meet and talk with engineers during visits to local engineering companies. Check with the college of engineering at a university near you to see if any summer programs are offered, or visit the Engineering Education Service Center's Web site at www. engineeringedu.com to find a camp in your area.

STUDENT COMPETITIONS

A great way to get a feel for engineering is to look at the student design competitions that are sponsored or co-sponsored by various engineering societies and organizations. These competitions are developed to encourage and motivate students. The competitions focus on teamwork and allow you to get a "real-world" feeling for the design process, including working with the cost of materials and team dynamics.

A few of the more popular competitions include
- Boosting Engineering, Science, and Technology (BEST). A robotic competition that provides students with an intense, hands-on, real engineering and problem-solving experience that is also fun. (www.bestinc.org)
- FIRST Robotics Competition. Corporations and

universities team up with high schools in a high-tech robot sporting event. (www.usfirst.org)

- Mathcounts. A national math coaching and competition program for 7th and 8th grade students. (www.mathcounts.org)
- Future City. Students learn about math and science in a challenging and interesting way through reality-based education using SimCity4 Deluxe software. (www.futurecity.org)
- International Bridge Building Contest. The construction and testing of model bridges promotes the study and application of fundamental principles of physics and also helps high-school students develop "hands-on" skills through bridge construction. By participating in the Bridge Building Competition students get a flavor of what it is to be an engineer by designing structures to a set of specifications, and then seeing how they perform. (www.iit.edu/~hsbridge)
- Odyssey of the Mind. A worldwide program that promotes creative team-based problem solving for kids from kindergarten through college. (www.odysseyofthemind.com)
- National Science Bowl. A U.S. Department of Energy academic competition where teams of high-school students answer questions on scientific topics in astronomy, biology, chemistry, mathematics, physics, earth, computer and general science. (www.scied.science.doe.gov/nsb)
- BattleBotsIQ. A comprehensive educational program where students learn about the science of engineering through robot building. This unique curriculum fuses mathematics, physics, and engineering into tangible and relevant lessons for high-school students. (www.battlebotsiq.com)

For a current and more comprehensive list of competitions, visit the Engineering Education Service Center's website: www. engineeringedu.com.

What Now?

Now that you have decided to pursue an engineering education, you should prepare for it as soon as possible. Search the Internet, and contact any societies that interest you. Browse their Web pages. Ask about their programs to help you prepare for college. Ask to talk to students currently participating in programs that interest you. Contact local engineering firms and ask for a tour. Most firms would be happy to show you around and explain what they do. Several companies encourage continuous improvement in engineering education. For example, a company may have a summer intern program that allows college-level science students to work at their facility each year. They may sponsor a job-shadow program to bring junior high and high school kids into the facilities or labs to see what their researchers are doing.

If you like the companies you've contacted, ask if they offer summer internships or job shadowing programs. Through this simple effort, you will make a contact, and more importantly, a potential job opportunity may await you when you finish your degree.

Choosing the Right School

Choosing the engineering school that is right for you is as important as wheels are to automobiles. Your choice should incorporate your preferences. The advantages and disadvantages of each school will depend on your personal needs and wants. Important considerations for most college-bound students include location, cost, faculty, school size, and academics.

1. Location: In addition to distance from home, location refers to the climate and the types of industry in the

surrounding area. If there is an industry specific to your degree, then opportunities for summer internships, co-op programs, and part-time work experience increase dramatically. These work experiences often lead to jobs after graduation.

2. Cost: Cost of attendance may be a critical factor in determining which school to select, although your decision should not be based on cost alone. Generally, public institutions are less expensive than private schools, but there are many ways to fund your education at any institution. Most engineering societies offer scholarships, and the government offers grants and loans. Part-time work, co-op programs, and campus jobs also help reduce the cost of attendance. Check with the financial aid department of the schools you are interested in to see what grants and loans you qualify for. Call the engineering department to find out about scholarships offered to incoming students through the college. The military may also offer opportunities for financing your education. The National Guard is a popular program among college students. The Air Force, U.S. Coast Guard, Marines, Merchant Marine, Army, and Navy offer education at reduced cost in exchange for a commitment to serve in the Armed Forces for a certain period of time.

3. Faculty: A fine faculty makes it easier to get a good education. A faculty that includes women and minorities will broaden your experience and better prepare you to work with people from diverse backgrounds. Faculty members can bring numerous experiences and expertise to their lectures. Check to make sure that faculty rather than graduate students teach the classes. As you proceed to your junior-level and senior-level classes, the research of the faculty becomes more important. Try to select a school that has at least one faculty member performing active research in your area of interest. That person can be a role model. You can talk and learn directly from

someone whose interests you share.

4. School Size: School size matters for some students. Large schools offer a greater diversity of people and more things to do, but often lack the professor-student interaction found at smaller schools. In a small school, you may get to know a larger percentage of classmates, but in a large school you can meet more people. You can receive an excellent education at a large school or a small one; which one you choose is purely a matter of preference.

5. Academics: Academics is probably the most important factor in choosing the school that's best for you. The program should be accredited by the Accreditation Board for Engineering and Technology (ABET). ABET accreditation ensures that the program follows national standards for faculty, curricula, students, administration, facilities, and institutional commitment. By choosing an ABET program, you can be sure that the faculty has met certain national standards and that the program is highly regarded by the profession. See the appendix for a list of ABET accredited schools.

Some students like the competitive atmosphere that accompanies attending a very prestigious school, and some students find they work better in a more relaxed environment. Both will  require a great deal of studying, although some programs will be more challenging than others. Pick the atmosphere that best fits your personality and aspirations. Questions you might ask yourself at this point include: Do I want to be on the cutting edge of technology? Do I want to find better solutions to existing identifiable problems (even if a current solution already exists)? Or do I want a combination of the two?

Some schools require their students to have computers, and other schools provide computer laboratories. Find out if free tutoring is offered and if the professors have posted office hours. Can you e-mail questions to professors? Will your questions be answered in a timely fashion? Another consideration is the campus library. Is it easy to find the information you are looking for? Does the school have a special engineering library or carry engineering journals?

Students frequently enjoy joining student chapters of professional organizations. These organizations can be an excellent resource during your college experience and in your career search. Many offer competitions against other colleges. Check to see if the society for the branch of engineering you want to study has student chapters at the schools you are considering.

Other school selection criteria to consider include sports facilities, leisure activities, community events, cultural events, and campus activities.

THE SUCCESSFUL STUDENT

Engineering is a rigorous and demanding major. To be successful in engineering school, you will need certain tools. You must be self-disciplined, organized, and manage your time effectively. In college, the "real" learning often takes place outside the classroom, and less time is spent in the classroom. A general rule of thumb is that for every hour spent in the classroom, engineering students can expect to spend three hours outside the classroom, compared with two hours for non-technical majors. A good time-management system can also allow you to participate in extracurricular activities, which broaden experience and are of interest to potential employers.

Engineering curricula vary from school to school; however, most schools don't require you to declare a specific field of interest until the end of your second year. The first two years of engineering school are focused on learning the fundamentals such as chemistry, calculus, physics, and mechanics such as statics and dynamics. Courses in English, the humanities, and biology are usually also required.

The third and fourth years of engineering school are most often spent studying your chosen specialty. Most universities require their students to complete a design project in their senior year. The project may be completed in teams or individually and solves a real-world problem. Students may be able to select a problem of personal interest, or local industry may present a problem they are currently exploring. Typically, the project requires a research report, the presentation of the design process, and an analysis of the results.

Co-ops and Internships

A cooperative, or co-op, educational experience is one where an engineering student alternates academics with work experience in government, industry, or business. For example, a student may do a parallel co-op where they work part-time and go to school part-time, or complete a traditional co-op where they work for six months and go to school for six months. A good co-op program may be the perfect answer for the non-traditional student who has financial responsibilities.

Because a co-op program usually takes longer to complete, your experience can be more meaningful. Additionally, a co-op experience can show employers that you have the experience and a solid desire to work in your chosen field. In today's competitive market, you need to do everything possible to stand out.

Engineering internships are another way to get your foot in the door. They generally consist of a summer job related to your major at an engineering company. David Tanaka of Industrial Light and Magic began his successful career by interning every summer. By the time he graduated, he was the first choice when a position became available. If you are interested in obtaining an internship position at an engineering firm, find a company you like and apply (send a resume) as early in the school year as possible.

EPICS (ENGINEERING PROJECTS IN COMMUNITY SERVICE)
EPICS teams undergraduates to design, build, and deploy real systems to solve engineering-based problems for local community service and education organizations. EPICS was founded and is headquatered at Purdue University.

EPICS programs are operating at 15 universities. Peer teams at multiple EPICS sites are collaborating to address community problems of national scope. EPICS appeals to people who want to make a difference in their community. High school EPICS programs are being created in Indiana, California, Massachusetts, and New York. (http://epics-high.ecn.purdue.edu/)

SUMMARY:
- Take as many engineering, math and science classes in high school as possible.
- Get involved in extracurricular activities such as robotics clubs.
- Practice your communication skills (speaking, writing and listening).
- Become well-rounded.
- Tour green engineering facilities such as wind towers or blade manufacturers, water treatment plants, or a LEED certified building companies.
- Enter engineering and technology competitions. When you win, it's very rewarding.
- Read everything you can about engineering to make sure it's the right career for you. This book is only one source of information and only mentions a few of the hundreds of things that you can do with an engineering career.
- Tour colleges of engineering. See what kinds of projects their students are doing, and try to figure out if you would enjoy going to school there. While on campus, talk to engineering students about their experiences and how

they decided to become an engineer.

- Take night and summer classes at your local community college. College-level classes are sometimes free for high school students. Take classes that are not offered at your high school, and focus on subjects that might be fun to learn about.
- Go to engineering camp, or seek opportunities for summer employment or internships with engineering firms or government research laboratories.
- Visit the U.S. Dept. of Labor Web site for information on career opportunities, growth trends, and salary ranges.

You are writing the script for your future and you should make it as interesting and engaging as possible.

Appendix

Glossary of Green Terms

Air pollution – contaminants or substances in the air that interfere with human health or produce other harmful environmental effects.

Alternative energy – usually environmentally friendly, this is energy from uncommon sources such as wind power or solar energy, not fossil fuels.

Alternative fuels – similar to above. Not petrol or diesel but different transportation fuels like natural gas, methanol, bio fuels and electricity.

Carbon Dioxide – Carbon dioxide (CO_2) is an atmospheric gas that is a major component of the carbon cycle. Although produced through natural processes, carbon dioxide is also released through human activities, such as the combustion of fossil fuels to produce electricity. Carbon dioxide is the predominate gas contributing to the greenhouse effect, and as such is known to contribute to climate change.

Carbon footprint – a measure of the your impact on the environment in terms of the amount of greenhouse gases produced, measured in units of carbon dioxide.

Carbon monoxide – a colourless, odourless and highly toxic gas commonly created during combustion.

Carbon neutral – a company, person or action either not producing any carbon emissions or if it does have been offsett elsewhere.

Climate – Climate in a narrow sense is usually defined as the "average weather," or more rigorously, as the statistical description in terms of the mean and variability of relevant quantities over a period of time ranging from months to thousands of years.

Climate change – a change in temperature and weather patterns due to human activity like burning fossil fuels.

Composting – a process whereby organic wastes, including food and paper, decompose naturally, resulting in a produce rich in minerals and ideal for gardening and farming as a soil conditioner, mulch, resurfacing material, or landfill cover.

Conservation – preserving and renewing, when possible, human and natural resources.

Emissions – The release of a substance (usually a gas when referring to the subject of climate change) into the atmosphere.

Energy Efficiency – Refers to products or systems using less energy to do the same or better job than conventional products or systems. Energy efficiency saves energy, saves money on utility bills, and helps protect the environment by reducing the demand for electricity. When buying or replacing products or appliances for your home, look for the ENERGY STAR® label.

Fossil Fuels – Fossil fuels are the nation's principal source of electricity. Fossil fuels come in three major forms: coal, oil, and natural gas. Because fossil fuels are a finite resource and cannot be replenished once they are extracted and burned, they are not considered renewable.

Fuel cell – a technology that uses an electrochemical process to convert energy into electrical power. Often powered by natural gas, fuel cell power is cleaner than grid-connected power sources. In addition, hot water is produced as a by-product.

Geothermal energy – heat that comes from the earth.

Global Climate Change – Climate change refers to any significant change in measures of climate (such as temperature, precipitation, or wind) lasting for an extended period (decades or longer). Climate change may result from:
  • Natural factors, such as changes in the sun's intensity or slow changes in the Earth's orbit around the sun
  • Natural processes within the climate system (e.g. ,changes in ocean circulation)
  • Human activities that change the atmosphere's composition (e.g., through burning fossil fuels) and the land surface (e.g., deforestation, reforestation, urbanization, desertification)

Green design – a design, usually architectural, conforming to environmentally sound principles of building, material and energy use. A green building, for example, might make use of solar panels, skylights, and recycled building materials.

Hydroelectric energy – electric energy produced by moving water.

Kilowatt-hour – A kilowatt-hour (kWh) is a standard metric unit of measurement for electricity.

Landfill – area where waste is dumped and eventually covered with dirt and topsoil.

Life cycle assessment – methodology developed to assess a product's full environmental costs, from raw material to final disposal.

Methane (CH4) – A hydrocarbon that is a greenhouse gas with a global warming potential most recently estimated at 23 times that of carbon dioxide (CO2). Methane is produced through anaerobic (without oxygen) decomposition of waste in landfills, animal digestion, decomposition of animal wastes, production and distribution of natural gas and petroleum, coal production, and incomplete fossil fuel combustion.

Non-renewable resources – Resources that are in limited supply, such as oil, coal, and natural gas.

Oil – fossil fuel used to produce gasoline and other materials such as plastics.

Organic – while it technically refers to molecules made up of two ore more atoms of carbon, it's generally now used as a term for the growth of vegetables etc without the use or artificial pesticides and fertilizer.

Photovoltaic panels – solar panels that convert sunlight into electricity. Power is produced when sunlight strikes the semiconductor material and creates an electrical current.

Recycling – the process of collecting, sorting, and reprocessing old material into usable raw materials.

Reduce – not using or buying products in the forst place so less waste, less recycling and less reusing.

Renewable Energy – The term renewable energy generally refers to electricity supplied from renewable energy sources, such as wind and solar power, geothermal, hydropower, and various forms of biomass. These energy sources are considered renewable sources because their fuel sources are continuously replenished.

Renewable resources – Like renewable energy, resources such as wind, waves, water, geothermal, sunlight and trees that regenerate.

Solar energy – energy from the sun.

Solar heating – heat from the sun is absorbed by collectors and transferred by pumps or fans to a storage unit for later use or to the house interior directly. Controls regulating the operation are needed. Or the heat can be transferred to water pumps for hot water.

WaterSense – a program sponsored by the U.S. Environmental Protection Agency (EPA), that is helping consumers identify high performance, water-efficient toilets that can reduce water use in the home and help preserve the nation's water resources.

Windpower – energy derived from the wind.

Bibliography/ Recommended Reading

AAUW: "Gender Gaps: Where Schools Still Fail Our Children," Washington, DC, 1998.

Astin, Alexander. What Matters in College?: Four Critical Years Revisited. San Francisco: Jossey-Bass, 1997.

Baine, Celeste. Is There an Engineer Inside You?: A Comprehensive Guide to Career Decisions in Engineering." Third Ed. Eugene, OR: Bonamy Publishing, 2011.

_____"Engineers Make a Difference: Motivating Student to Pursue an Engineering Education." Eugne, OR: Bonamy Publishing, 2008.

————. "Ideas in Action: A Girl's Guide to Careers in Engineering." Eugne, OR: Bonamy Publishing, 2009.

————. "The Musical Engineer: A Music Enthusiast's Guide to Careers in Music Engineering and Technology." Eugene, OR: Bonamy Publishing, 2007.

————. "The Maritime Engineer: Careers in Naval Architecture and Marine, Ocean and Naval Engineering." Eugene, OR: Bonamy Publishing, 2010.

————. "The Fantastical Engineer: A Thrillseeker's Guide to Careers in Theme Park Engineering." Second Ed. Eugene, OR: Bonamy Publishing, 2007.

————. "High Tech Hot Shots: Careers in Sports Engineering." Alexandria, VA: National Society of Professional Engineers, 2004.

Belcher, M. Clay. "What is Architectural Engineering?" University of Kansas Press, 1993.

Bolles, Richard Nelson. What Color is your Parachute?: A Practical Manual for Job Hunters and Career Changers. Berkeley: Ten Speed Press, 2001.

Brockman, Reed. From Sundaes to Space Stations: Careers in Civil Engineering. Eugene, OR: Bonamy Publishing, 2010.

Bronyn a Llewellyn, K. C. Golden, James P. Hendrix Ph.D. "Green Jobs: A Guide to Eco-Friendly Employment." Avon, MA. Adams Media.2008.

"Careers in Science and Engineering: A Student Guide to Grad School and Beyond." National Academy Press, 1996.

Carnegie, Dale. How to Win Friends and Influence People. New York: Simon & Schuster, 1994.

Catsambis, S. "The Path to Math: Gender and Racial-Ethnic Differences in Mathematics Participation From Middle to High School," Sociology of Education 67 (1994): pp. 199-215.

Congressional Commission on the Advancement of Women and Minorities in Science Engineering and Technology Development, "Land of Plenty," Arlington, VA, Sept. 2000.

Etzkowitz, Henry, Carol Kemelgor, and Michael Neuschatz. "Barriers to Women in Academic Science and Engineering." Baltimore: John Hopkins University Press, 1994.

Ferguson, Eugene S. Enginering and the Mind's Eye. Cambridge: MIT Press, 1997.

Ferrell, Tom. Peterson's Job Opportunities for Engineering and Computer Science Majors. United States: Thomson Learning, 1999.

Florman, Samual C. The Introspective Engineer. New York: St. Martin's Press, 1996.

Gabelman, Irving. "The New Engineer's Guide to Career Growth and Professional Awareness." New York: IEEE Press, 1996.

"The Green Report: Engineering Education for a Changing World." American Society for Engineering Education, 1998.

Landis, Raymond B. Studying Engineering: A Roadmap to a Rewarding Career. Burbank, CA: Discovery Press, 1995.

————. "Enhancing Student Success: A Five Step Process for Getting Students to 'Study Smart'." American Society for Engineering Education, Washington, DC, 1998.

————. "Enhancing Engineering Student Success: A Pedagogy for Changing Behaviors." American Society for Engineering Education, Washington, DC, 1997.

LeBold, William K. and Dona J. LeBold. "Women Engineers: A Historical Perspective." American Society for Engineering Education, Washington, DC, 1998.

Love, Sydney F. Planning and Creating Successful Engineered Designs: Managing the Design Process. Los Angeles: Advanced Professional Development Incorporated, 1986.

Morgan, Robert P. Proctor P. Reid, and Wm, A. Wulf, "The Changing Nature of Engineering." ASEE PRISM, May-June 1998.

The National Science Foundation. "Women, Minorities and Persons with Disabilities in Science and Engineering: 2000." Washington, DC, Sept. 2000.

National Society of Professional Engineers: "The NSPE 2001 Income and Salary Survey." Alexandria, VA: 2001.

Peters, Robert L. Getting What You Came For: The Smart Student's Guide to Earning a Master's or Ph.D. New York: Farrar, Straus and Giroux,

1997.

Peterson, George D. "Engineering Criteria 2000: A Bold New Change Agent." American Society for Engineering Education, Washington, DC, 1998.

Petroski, Henry. Invention by Design: How Engineers Get from Thought to Thing. Cambridge: Harvard University Press, 1996.

————. To Engineer is Human: The Role of Failure in Successful Design. New York: Vintage Books, 1992.

————. The Evolution of Useful Things: How Everyday Artifacts-From Forks and Pins to Paper Clips and Zippers-Came to be as They Are. New York: Vintage Books, 1992.

"Planning a Career in Biomedical Engineering." Biomedical Engineering Society, Baltimore, 1996.

Sherwood, Kaitlin. "Women in the Engineering Industry." Society of Women Engineers at UIUC lecture, 1994.

"Simple Machines." Society of Women Engineers Career Guidance Module, Chicago, 1996.

"Student Science Training Programs for Precollege Students." Science Service, Inc., New York, 1994.

Tieger, Paul and Barbara Barron-Tieger. Do What You Are: Discover the Perfect Career for You through the Secrets of Personality Type. Boston: Little, Brown and Company, 1995.

Tietsen, Jill S. and Kristy A Schloss with Carter, Bishop, and Kravits. Keys to Engineering Success. New Jersey: Prentice Hall, 2001.

U.S. Labor Statistics: JOBS 2000.

Vanderheiden, Gregg. "Thirty Something (Million): Should There Be Exceptions?" Trace Research and Development Center, Waisman Center and Department of Industrial Engineering, University of Wisconsin-Madison, 1996.

"Women, Minorities, and Persons with Disabilities in Science and Engineering: 1996," The National Science Foundation, Washington, DC, 1996.

Yantzi, Lindsay. "The Construction Industry's Orthopedic Specialist." University of Kansas-Lawrence, 1997.

Websites to Visit

National Renewable Energy Lab (NREL) -www.nrel.gov
National Council for Science and the Environment-www.cnie.org
Pacific Northwest Pollution Prevention Research Center-www.pprc.org
U.S. Environmnetal Protection Agency - Green Engineering -www.epa.gov
National Renewable Energy Lab (NREL) -www.nrel.gov
National Council for Science and the Environment-www.cnie.org
Pacific Northwest Pollution Prevention Research Center-www.pprc.org
U.S. Department of Energy-www.doe.gov
U.S. Environmental Protection Agency-www.epa.gov
U.S. Geological Survey-www.usgs.gov
American Chemical Society Green Chemistry Institute-www.chemistry.org
Center for Energy Efficiency and Renewable Technologies-www.cleanpower.org
Environmental Health News-www.environmentalhealthnews.org
Environmental News Network-www.enn.com
Local Governments for Sustainability-www.iclei.org
Global Network for Environmental Technology - GNET-www.gnest.org
National Center for Environmental Research-www.epa.gov
The Natural Step-www.naturalstep.org
Recycler's World-www.recycle.net
Rocky Mountain Institute-www.rmi.org
United Nations Environment Program - Life Cycle Analysis-www.uneptie.org
US Green Building Council-www.usgbc.org

Schools

AGRICULTURAL ENGINEERING
Auburn University, Auburn, AL, US
California Polytechnic State University, San Luis Obispo, San Luis Obispo, CA, US
Clemson University, Clemson, SC, US
Florida A & M University, Tallahassee, FL, US
Iowa State University, Ames, IA, US
Kansas State University, Manhattan, KS, US
Louisiana State University and A&M College, Baton Rouge, LA, US
Michigan State University, East Lansing, MI, US
North Carolina State University at Raleigh, Raleigh, NC, US
North Dakota State University, Fargo, ND, US
Oklahoma State University, Stillwater, OK, US
Oregon State University, Corvallis, OR, US
Purdue University at West Lafayette, West Lafayette, IN, US
South Dakota State University, Brookings, SD, US
State University of New York College of Environmental Science and Forestry, Syracuse, NY, US
Texas A & M University, College Station, TX, US
The Ohio State University (Formerly Ohio State University), Columbus, OH, US
University of Arkansas, Fayetteville, AR, US
University of California, Davis, Davis, CA, US
University of Florida, Gainesville, FL, US
University of Georgia, Athens, GA, US
University of Idaho, Moscow, ID, US
University of Illinois at Urbana-Champaign, Urbana, IL, US
University of Kentucky, Lexington, KY, US
University of Maine, Orono, ME, US
University of Nebraska-Lincoln, Lincoln, NE, US
University of Tennessee at Knoxville, Knoxville, TN, US
University of Wisconsin-Madison, Madison, WI, US
Utah State University, Logan, UT, US
Virginia Polytechnic Institute and State University, Blacksburg, VA, US

ENVIRONMENTAL ENGINEERING
California Polytechnic State University, San Luis Obispo, San Luis Obispo, CA, US
City University of New York, City College, New York, NY, US
Clarkson University, Potsdam, NY, US
Colorado State University, Fort Collins, CO, US
Columbia University, New York, NY, US
Cornell University, Ithaca, NY, US
Drexel University, Philadelphia, PA, US
Florida Gulf Coast University, Fort Myers, FL, US
Florida International University (Modesto Maidique Campus), Miami, FL, US
Gannon University, Erie, PA, US
Georgia Institute of Technology, Atlanta, GA, US
Humboldt State University ,Arcata, CA, US
Lehigh University, Bethlehem, PA, US
Louisiana State University and A&M College, Baton Rouge, LA, US
Manhattan College, Riverdale, NY, US
Massachusetts Institute of Technology, Cambridge, MA, US
Michigan Technological University, Houghton, MI, US
Missouri University of Science and Technology, Rolla, MO, US
Montana Tech of the University of Montana, Butte, MT, US
New Mexico Institute of Mining and Technology, Socorro, NM, US
North Carolina State University at Raleigh, Raleigh, NC, US
Northern Arizona University, Flagstaff, AZ, US
Northwestern University, Evanston, IL, US
Old Dominion University, Norfolk, VA, US
Oregon State University, Corvallis, OR, US
Pennsylvania State University, University Park, PA, US

Pennsylvania State University, Harrisburg, The Capital College, Middletown, PA, US
Rensselaer Polytechnic Institute, Troy, NY, US
Rutgers, The State University of New Jersey, New Brunswick, NJ, US
San Diego State University, San Diego, CA, US
South Dakota School of Mines and Technology, Rapid City, SD, US
Southern Methodist University, Dallas, TX, US
Stanford University, Stanford, CA, US
State University of New York at Buffalo, Buffalo, NY, US
Stevens Institute of Technology, Hoboken, NJ, US
University of Nevada-Reno, Reno, NV, US
University of New Hampshire, Manchester, NH, US
University of Oklahoma (Formerly University of Oklahoma), Norman, OK, US
University of Southern California, Los Angeles, CA, US
University of Vermont, Burlington, VT, US
University of Wisconsin-Platteville, Platteville, WI, US
Utah State University, Logan, UT, US
Wilkes University, Wilkes-Barre, PA, US
Worcester Polytechnic Institute, Worcester, MA, US

GEOLOGICAL ENGINEERING
Colorado School of Mines, Golden, CO, US
Michigan Technological University, Houghton, MI, US
Missouri University of Science and Technology, Rolla, MO, US
Montana Tech of the University of Montana, Butte, MT, US
South Dakota School of Mines and Technology, Rapid City, SD, US
University of Alaska Fairbanks, Fairbanks, AK, US
University of Minnesota-Twin Cities, Minnesota, MN, US
University of Mississippi, University, MS, US
University of Nevada-Reno, Reno, NV, US
University of North Dakota, Grand Forks, ND, US
University of Texas at Austin, Austin, TX, US
University of Utah, Salt Lake City, UT, US
University of Wisconsin-Madison, Madison, WI, US

SOLAR ENERGY
Appalachian State University, Boone, NC
Lane Community College, Eugene, OR
San Juan College, Farmington, NM
North Carolina State University, Raleigh, NC

SUSTAINABILITY ENGINEERING
University of Illinois, Champaign, IL

RENEWABLE ENERGY
Oregon Institute of Technology, Portland, OR
Saint Francis University, Loretto, PA

WIND ENERGY
Texas Tech University Wind Science and Engineering Research Center
University of Massachusetts Center for Energy Efficiency and Renewable Energy
University of Utah Wind Energy Research Program
MIT Laboratory for Energy and the Environment
Illinois Institute of Technology Energy and Sustainability Institute

UNIVERSITIES AND CENTERS
California Polytechnic State Unversity - Center for Sustainability in Engineering
Carnegie Mellon University Green Design Initiative
Center for Sustainable Engineering - Carnegie Mellon, University of Texas-Austin, Arizona State
Georgia Tech - Institute for Sustainable Technology and Development

Michigan Tech - Sustainable Futures Institute
University of Massachusetts Lowell - Center for Green Chemistry
University of Michigan - Center for Sustainable Systems (Factsheets are excellent resource)
University of Michigan - Program in the Environment
University of Oregon - Green Chemistry
University of Pittsburgh - The Mascaro Sustainability Initiative
Penn State Institutes of the Environment
Stanford University - Civil and Environmental Engineering Department
Stanford University - Woods Institute for the Environment

ABOUT THE AUTHOR

Celeste Baine is a biomedical engineer, Director of the Engineering Education Service Center and the award-winning author of over twenty books and booklets on engineering careers and education. She won the Norm Augustine Award from the National Academy of Engineering (The Norm Augustine award is given to an engineer who has demonstrated the capacity for communicating the excitement and wonder of engineering). She also won the American Society for Engineering Education's Engineering Dean Council's Award for the Promotion of Engineering Education and Careers, and is listed on the National Engineers Week website as one of 50 engineers you should meet. The National Academy of Engineering has included Celeste in their Gallery of Women Engineers and she has been named one of the Nifty-Fifty individuals who have made a major impact on the field of engineering by the USA Science and Engineering Festival. She has spent the past decade advising students and parents on the challenges and benefits of obtaining an engineering degree.

Other Engineering Career Publications by
Celeste Baine

Is There an Engineer Inside You? A Comprehensive Guide to Career Decisions in Engineering. Third Edition $24.95

Engineers Make a Difference: Motivating Students to Pursue an Engineering Education. $21.95

The Musical Engineer: A Music Enthusiast's Guide to Engineering and Technology Careers. $17.95

The Fantastical Engineer: A Thrillseeker's Guide to Careers in Theme Park Engineering. Second Edition. $17.95

High Tech Hot Shots: Careers in Sports Engineering. $19.95

Ideas in Action: A Girl's Guide to Careers in Engineering $7.95

Is There a Civil Engineer Inside You? A Student's Guide to Exploring Careers in Civil Engineering & Civil Engineering Technology. $7.95

Is There a Computer Engineer Inside You? A Student's Guide to Exploring Careers in Computer Engineering & Computer Engineering Technology. $7.95

Is There a Mechanical Engineer Inside You? A Student's Guide to Exploring Careers in Mechanical Engineering & Mechanical Engineering Technology. $7.95

Is There a Chemical Engineer Inside You? A Student's Guide to Exploring Careers in Chemical Engineering. $7.95

Is There a Biomedical Engineer Inside You? A Student's Guide to Exploring Careers in Biomedical Engineering & Biomedical Engineering Technology. $7.95

Is There an Electrical Engineer Inside You? A Student's Guide to Exploring Careers in Electrical Engineering & Electrical Engineering Technology. $7.95

Is There a Manufacturing Engineer Inside You? A Student's Guide to Exploring Careers in Manufacturing Engineering & Manufacturing Engineering Technology. $7.95

To Order:
call 1-541-988-1005 tel, Fax orders to 1-541-988-1008
Online orders www.engineeringedu.com